SPEED
TO
MARKET

Second Edition

LEAN MANUFACTURING
FOR JOB SHOPS

VINCENT BOZZONE

AMACOM
American Management Association

New York • Atlanta • Chicago • Kansas City • San Francisco • Washington, D.C.
Brussels • Mexico City • Tokyo • Toronto

Special discounts on bulk quantities of AMACOM books are available to corporations, professional associations, and other organizations. For details, contact Special Sales Department, AMACOM, a division of American Management Association, 1601 Broadway, New York, NY 10019.
Tel.: 212-903-8316.   Fax: 212-903-8083.
Web site: www. amacombooks.org

This publication is designed to provide accurate and authoritative information in regard to the subject matter covered. It is sold with the understanding that the publisher is not engaged in rendering legal, accounting, or other professional service. If legal advice or other expert assistance is required, the services of a competent professional person should be sought.

Library of Congress Cataloging-in-Publication Data

Bozzone, Vincent.
    Speed to market : lean manufacturing for job shops / Vincent Bozzone.—2nd ed.
    p. cm.
  Includes bibliographical references and index.
  ISBN 0-8144-0694-7
  1. Production management. 2. Production schedule. I. Title.

TS155 .B615 2001
658.5—dc21

2001037308

Printing number

10 9 8 7 6 5 4 3 2

In memory of
Harvey W. Wallender III,
friend and collaborator

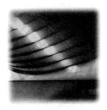

CONTENTS

FOREWORD

The days when price and quality were the only factors taken into account when choosing a vendor are over. Today, quality is a given if you expect to remain a player in any competitive market, and price alone can't make up for the lost opportunities that long lead times create. A huge competitive advantage exists when one player can outperform the rest of the pack by delivering quality products or services at a value the customer feels is justified . . . and with the shortest lead time. The race to win orders begins when a customer's need is discovered and ends when he or she has the merchandise in hand. The clock is running during every activity that occurs in between.

After having spent more than thirty years in manufacturing, I can vividly remember the days when the usual excuse for a missed delivery promise was that we hadn't been given enough lead time. Everything revolved around throwing an order out on the shop floor and hoping for the best. Unfortunately, the floor was already overburdened with more work than could possibly be processed within the expected time frame. Work in process far outweighed short-term capacity. No one had the time or authority to cross over functional lines to investigate all the blockages that were preventing upstream tasks from being processed in the most expedient manner, and it was not unusual for orders to hit the floor after the promised delivery date had come and gone!

Responsibility for missed delivery promises fell on the shoulders of the expediters who were swamped with paperwork, schedules, hot lists, constant customer complaints, and delivery changes. In those days, we believed that lead-time reductions could only come from the shop floor. Now with the advantage provided by process analysis, we know that the shop is only one link in the lead-time chain, and that every link needs to be investigated and improved to get that product into the customer's hands as quickly as possible.

Potential orders are often won or lost within a short time. Being first to respond to a customer's inquiry, promising the quickest delivery of the product, or responding first to a customer's request for a quotation are very powerful tools. You stand an excellent chance of capturing an order during your first contact with a customer when you respond quickly and when you can promise—and deliver—in the shortest possible time. Each "I'll get back to you" opens the door for a competitor to sneak past. Think of how many times you chose a supplier because he or she could deliver more quickly than his or her competitors, not because the price was less.

What kind of lead-time reduction can you expect? If you haven't implemented any kind of lead-time reduction effort, I'd estimate you have a potential of cutting 75 percent or more off your lead time (customer contact to product delivery). Today, my company can make and ship a made-to-order product in less time than it used to take us to get an order through order entry and out to the floor. This is a tremendous competitive advantage that we see reflected in our sales and profit figures . . . and we're not done yet! Opportunities await any organization that is willing to look deep enough into itself, ask the right questions, and make changes to "the way it's always been done around here."

Speed To Market provides you with a comprehensive, practical guide for reducing your lead time, responding to customers' needs more quickly, and improving the operating and financial performance of your company. I'm pleased to be able to introduce this valuable book to you.

—KEN RIZNER
VICE PRESIDENT, MANUFACTURING
HYDE TOOLS
SOUTHBRIDGE, MASSACHUSETTS

AUTHOR'S INTRODUCTION

Whether you call it lean manufacturing, quick-response manufacturing, cycle-time compression, speed to market, or whatever other terms you choose, improving performance and profitability in job shops and custom manufacturing businesses boils down to cutting lead time. This is the single, most effective strategy you can follow to strengthen your company's competitive position, increase profits, and secure the future of your business—bar none. Cutting lead time—or more accurately, customer wait time—is the essence of lean manufacturing in make-to-order manufacturing businesses. When you eliminate delays that prevent you from serving customers more quickly, your business will grow and prosper. Guaranteed! Profitable growth, not reducing inventories, is the mother lode in a job shop environment, and this book will show you how to mine it!

Part I

Lean manufacturing has become a popular methodology many companies are using to drive out waste, increase value to customers, increase profitability, and become more competitive. Be advised, however, that the philosophy and principles of lean manufacturing originated in mass-production manufacturing and so must be redefined before they can be applied successfully in job shops and custom manufacturing environments. Attempting to implement lean programs without understanding these differences can actually increase your costs, and will not produce the results you expect. The essential differences between lean programs in mass and custom manufacturing are explained in Chapter 1.

Although many companies approach the challenge of reducing lead time by focusing almost exclusively on manufacturing while ignoring the rest of the organization, the enterprisewide view presented in this book enables you to recognize the many opportunities for reducing lead time that exists throughout your company. Chapters 2 through 4 show you how to look at your business as a process, and how to apply the lean principles of pull, flow, and the elimination of waste *(muda)* from "quotes to cash." Eliminating delays in your business process will increase sales, reduce work-in-process, cut costs, improve margins, accelerate cash flow, and increase effective production capacity all at the same time.

One of the most important steps you can take to position your company for profitable growth is to ensure that your business is properly aligned with its markets and customers. Chapter 5 uses the concept of value streams as a basis for organization, as well as describes methods for eliminating delays and improving performance on the floor.

Continuous improvement is based on the fact that perfection is an ideal, so anything and everything can be improved. It is a key concept in lean manufacturing in combination with pull, flow, and the elimination of waste or *muda*. Chapter 6 describes how to put a nonbureaucratic continuous improvement process to work in your company.

The manufacturing environment has undergone a major paradigm change during the past thirty years or so, and continues to evolve. We have seen a transformation from rich to lean, push to pull, just-in-case to just-in-time, in-house to outsourced, and top down command-and-control to self-managing, horizontal process teams. Suppliers operating in this environment must improve continuously and adapt more efficiently to remain competitive and survive.

This means companies can no longer view implementation as the weak link in improving performance, but must take steps to learn how to implement more quickly and efficiently. I've had a great deal of experience implementing literally hundreds of performance- and profit-improvement programs, and those readers who are serious about making their businesses perform better can benefit from this hard-earned knowledge. Chapter 7 addresses the difficulties of implementation in detail: why they fail and what you can do to be more successful.

Part II

There is no question that certain types of problems are created or intensified in job shops when concepts derived from mass-production manufacturing are mistakenly applied to managing these types of make-to-order businesses. Job shops operate on a completely different operational and business model compared to volume production, build-to-stock manufacturing. Just because they are both called manufacturing does not mean they can be viewed and managed in the same way or with the same concepts. That would be like saying you can drive a car and fly a plane the same way because they are both means of transportation.

The five chapters in Part II build on this theme. Common job shop problems that result from using the wrong concepts are explored. "Wrong concepts" in this case refers to using mass-production manufacturing ideas in a job shop environment where they don't fit, don't work, and become a major organizational distraction.

Chapter 8, "When Scheduling Is Out of Control," shows that the concept of static scheduling, which is suitable in more stable mass-production operations, is the wrong paradigm for a dynamic job shop environment. The concept of dynamic scheduling is introduced, as well as other steps you can take to get scheduling under control.

Hockey stick is a term used to describe a pattern common to job shops in which a great effort is expended during the last week of the month to ship as much as possible to "make the numbers." The hockey stick image represents the pattern of more or less equal shipments during the first three weeks of the month with a big spike at the end. Chapter 9 examines the hockey stick pattern in more depth, by offering some insight into its dynamics and showing how it can be ameliorated. You may not be able to eliminate it completely, but you can make it less severe, less disruptive, and less costly.

The question of how to allocate overhead is a thorny issue for many job shops. It is important because overhead is a significant portion of the cost structure, and consequently the price quoted to a customer. Using labor or machine hours as a basis for allocation is not always appropriate or accurate due to their variability. Chapter 10 discusses the limitations of these traditional (mass-production) allocation bases, and offers a new perspective and approach for this common job shop dilemma.

Part III

The Appendixes in the "Tools of the Trade" section present a selection of practical concepts, process analysis tools, and perspective-enhancing techniques that you can use immediately to improve performance and profitability. These are in addition to those presented throughout the book. You may find it worthwhile to complete the survey, "Is This Your Shop?" (see Appendix A). Completing this survey and reviewing the accompanying Item Analysis will give you a good idea how your business can benefit directly from the perspective, strategies, and information presented in this book.

A Note on Job Shops

Job shops and made-to-order custom manufacturers are the unsung heroes and backbone of U.S. industry. Without the specialized skills and on-demand services these companies provide to larger enterprises, industry would not exist in the United States as we know it today. Take the job shops out of any large company's supplier base, and the whole thing would come down like a house of cards. At the same time, the vital role job shops play in enabling larger companies to compete successfully in the global economy is generally not well-recognized or appreciated.

As a former job shop owner and business consultant who has worked in some three hundred companies in a wide variety of industries over the last twenty years, I've found that job shops are the most difficult of all types of manufacturing operations to manage. They are infinitely variable, and the differences among them are significant. Some shops work with flat plates; others with three-dimensional parts; others use the latest CNC machining technology; others injection-mold plastics, aluminum, and alloys of all types; others blend custom chemicals. Some are foundries; some cut and sew clothing; some require extensive hand-assembly operations; others make glass items. The variations are endless. This book focuses on what they have in common, not their differences.

They also tend to be comparatively small—the vast majority have fewer than one hundred people with annual revenues of less than $10 million. Many are only marginally profitable with any available reinvestment capital generally being spent on production equipment and machinery, rather than on the people and organizational side of the business. Most are being squeezed by their customers to cut costs, improve quality, and deliver more quickly. Many lack the resources and expertise required to meet these increasing demands, and have no organized approach for improving organizational performance.

Unfortunately, these types of businesses are not getting much help. Even though there are literally thousands of management books written on every conceivable topic, I could not find anything in the popular management literature that dealt specifically with how to manage and bring about performance improvement in a custom manufacturing environment when the first edition of *Speed to Market* was published in 1998.

No book is the work of a single individual, and I would like to thank Ron Fowler, editor and publisher of *Metal Fabricating News* for publishing the original series of articles that ultimately led to this book. The many favorable calls and comments received from readers suggested that a guidebook for improving performance in job shops was sorely needed and would be favorably received.

Chris Emmons, president of Human Resource Professionals of Detroit, read previous versions of the manuscript and provided perspective and help in organizing the content. My sister, Dorothy Bozzone, edited previous versions of the manuscript, made many helpful suggestions, and pushed the writing forward at a time when it was most needed. Mr. Donald F. Utter, senior organization design consultant, Lucent Technologies, enhanced this book with his thoughtful critiques. Rick Cloutier, national sales manager for Hyde Tools, collected the data and performed the analysis that shows how important it is to respond to requests for quotations quickly (see Chapter 3).

Hyde Tools deserves special recognition. They funded and enthusiastically supported projects that led to the development of the approach described in this book, and have been most generous in allowing me to share the results of my work with them to others. Ken Rizner, Hyde's vice president of engineered products, read and reread the manuscript, and provided much valuable support along the way. I am also indebted to the many teachers, clients, and colleagues from whom I have learned a great deal.

My family deserves special recognition for their support, and for putting up with the vagaries that come with a writing and consulting lifestyle.

If you are truly motivated and committed to making your business grow and prosper, I know you will find *Speed to Market* invaluable in providing you with a wide-ranging set of concepts, insights, tools, and techniques you can apply immediately to increase your speed to market, solve problems, make your organization work better, improve your bottom line, and get you going on the golden road to profitable growth.

Hopefully, this book will help free job shop owners and managers from the tyranny of mass-production thinking, and will confirm what most already know: that managing a job shop is different.

—Vincent Bozzone
Bloomfield Hills, Michigan

SPEED TO MARKET

Second Edition

PART I

SPEED TO MARKET

CHAPTER ONE

LEAPFROGGING LEAN

Many companies are pursuing lean manufacturing programs to drive out waste, increase value to customers, improve profitability, and become more competitive. However, it is important to recognize that concepts and methods of lean manufacturing are derived from mass-production operations, and must be adapted to job shops and custom manufacturing environments before they can be applied successfully. An expensive lesson is in store for job shops that do not understand the difference. A careful reading of Chapter 1 will enable you to make better decisions when it comes to implementing lean manufacturing in your company.

What Is Lean Manufacturing?

Lean manufacturing is a strategy for performance improvement based on concepts and methods derived from Taiichi Ohno's revamping of Toyota's production system some thirty years ago.[1] He recognized that waste is inherent in inventories, and set about finding ways to make Toyota's production system leaner. The practice of lean manufacturing has come to include Japanese terms such as *kaikaku* (radical improvement), *kaizen* (continuous improvement), *muda* (waste), *poke-a-yoke* (mistake proofing), *kan-ban* (material control cards), and other concepts and methods for improving organizational performance and productivity. The key concepts that comprise the lean manufacturing system are pull, flow, the elimination of waste (*muda*), and continuous improvement.

A Note on Terminology: The terms *mass production business, volume manufacturing operation,* and *build-to-stock business* are all used interchangeably. The term *job shop* is used to refer to all types of custom manufacturing, make-to-order businesses (not only machine shops) that meet the following four criteria:

1. Produce on an order-by-order basis to meet customers' specifications (that is, are order driven).
2. Secure work through a bidding process.
3. Serve other companies and/or distributors as opposed to consumers or end users.
4. Are service companies.

The characteristic of being a service company may not be fully recognized because the primary focus of company attention is on the manufacturing technology employed. However, those companies that truly understand they are in a service business will be in the best position to exploit speed to market as a competitive advantage.

The Concept of Pull

The idea inherent in *pull* is for actual customer demand to drive the manufacturing process as much as possible. The closer production output can match actual customer orders, the better. When supply and demand are more closely aligned, inventories throughout the system are reduced (especially finished goods inventories). The primary objective of any lean program in a mass-production operation is to minimize inventories that are being built on the basis of projected demand.

In a push system, on the other hand, production is *disconnected* from actual customer orders. Finished goods inventories are built on the basis of a forecast that is actually a demand projection. When orders do not materialize as forecasted, or the demand mix changes, waste is created (unsold inventory or lost sales). In a pull system, less inventory is built on spec, so to speak, which reduces carrying costs. This amount is normally in the 20- to 30-percent range of the total inventory investment (for example, about \$250,000 annually for every \$1,000,000 in inventory). Reducing this cost has a direct impact on bottom-line profitability, so it makes sense to go after it, and lean manufacturing is the strategy of choice for improvement.

The article "A Mouse Click, a Car Built: Web May Help Automakers Custom-build Cars in 5 Days" clearly illustrates the difference between push and pull systems.

This article from *The Detroit News*[2] reports that consumers will be able to specify exactly what combination of features and options they want in a new car over the Internet. The car would then be custom-built to their specifications at the factory, and delivered to them within five days instead of the current norm of several weeks. Thus, an automaker would be building cars based on actual customer orders (pull), and not flooding dealer's lots with inventory (push) based on a forecast. The more that auto production is based on actual orders (pull), the less would need to be pushed, and the lower the level of dealers' inventories and carrying costs would become. Theoretically, this system will benefit consumers.

Leapfrogging Lean

Job shops already work on a pull system. In job shops and customer manufacturing, nothing is produced until an order is received. That is the nature of a make-to-order business. So if the objective of lean manufacturing is to make a mass-production system operate like a job shop, how does lean manufacturing apply in job shops where that objective has already been achieved?

Most of what we have learned about manufacturing management is derived from mass-production operations, and virtually all management education assumes mass production to be the standard manufacturing model. Little or no attention is given to the unique requirements of job shops and custom manufacturing, and these types of companies are mostly ignored in the management literature. Table 1-1 illustrates important differences between them.

Table 1-1. Differences between job shops and mass production manufactur-

Job Shops	Mass Production
• Make to order/custom	• Build to stock
• No finished goods inventories	• Finished goods inventories/SKUs
• Different products	• Standard products
• Sell to other companies	• Sell to distributors or end users
• Customer order-driven	• MRP demand forecast-driven
• Bid on RFQs to get work	• No RFQs
• Estimating is critical	• Standard costing
• Customer pricing (quotes)	• Market pricing
• Lead time required	• Fill orders from finished goods inventory
• Many schedule changes	• Fewer schedule changes
• Setups/changeovers frequent	• Setups/changeovers less frequent
• Direct contact with customer	• Indirect contact with remote customer
• Smaller companies	• Larger companies
• Owner managed	• "Professionally" managed
• Variable overhead allocation	• Labor-based overhead allocation
• Variable volume	• More stable volume
• Order backlog is good	• Order backlog is bad (stock outs)
• More dynamic	• More static
• More skilled labor (variable tasks)	• Less skilled labor (repetitive tasks)
• Dynamic scheduling	• Level scheduling
• Shorter runs	• Longer runs
• Improve by reducing lead time	• Improve by reducing inventories

Clearly, these are fundamentally different manufacturing systems. You cannot expect a lean manufacturing program, which may work well in a mass-production business, to work in a custom manufacturing environment.

Muda is the Japanese word for waste. The most expensive type of waste in a mass-production system is making and inventorying products for which no customer demand exists. (This was Taiichi Ohno's great insight that led to the development of lean manufacturing at Toyota.) However, when the concepts of pull and flow are brought together in a lean manufacturing strategy, excess inventories—especially finished goods—are squeezed out of the production system, and a major source of *muda* is minimized or eliminated. (Unsold cars sitting on a dealer's lot are defined as *muda* in lean manufacturing terms.)

The Concept of Flow

Flow is accomplished operationally through flexible manufacturing—small lot sizes, quick changeovers, dedicated cells, *kan-ban* systems, just-in-time scheduling, and a variety of other methods designed to make a mass-production system more readily adaptable to fluctuations in market and customer demand. Flexible manufacturing enables products to flow through the system in smaller lot sizes with greater variety. In this way, production is able to mirror actual demand more closely, so there is less need for inventory in the system.

Flexibility in manufacturing also shortens the forecasting horizon, which results in greater accuracy. It is much easier to predict what is going to happen tomorrow that it is to predict even a week from now. This combination of flexible manufacturing and a shortened forecasting window further reduces the need to build and maintain expensive finished goods inventories that act as a buffer between mismatched demand and supply.

The Concept of Continuous Improvement

Finding new ways to serve customers more efficiently—and at a higher service level—is not something you do; rather something you keep doing, and that is where continuous improvement comes in. The concept of continuous improvement is based on the fact that perfection is an ideal, so anything and everything can be improved. It is a philosophical stance that makes sense in today's business world, where fast-paced change, new technologies, and more demanding competitive pressures prevail. Continuous improvement is antithetical to the "If it ain't broke, don't fix it" mentality, and these contradictory orientations are often a source of organizational conflict.

Lean Manufacturing in Job Shops

The same key concepts of pull, flow, *muda*, and continuous improvement apply in job shops, but not in the same way. We've already noted that a job shop works on a pull system because it makes to order, and does not build finished goods inventories. Further, if the solution for *muda* in a mass-production operation is to run more like a job shop, then logic dictates that excess inventory cannot be a major source of waste in a job shop where this solution is already employed. *In other words, the lean strategy of driving out waste by minimizing or eliminating inventories does not apply in a job shop or custom manufacturing environments.* This does not mean there is no waste in a job shop; it's just not in the form of excess inventory. The mother lode lies elsewhere.

The Essential Difference

A subtle and yet profound difference between lean in these two types of manufacturing systems lies in how supply and demand are brought together. In a mass-production system, the lean strategy is product-based. Meeting actual orders for products while minimizing inventories is accomplished through flexible manufacturing (that is, small lot sizes, quick changeovers, dedicated cells, or *kan-ban* systems, as noted previously). The basic idea is: Make what you can sell, don't make what you can't sell, and don't lose sales because you failed to make what you could have sold.

In a job shop, matching supply and demand is not product-based (a job shop only makes what the customer has already ordered, so product demand and supply are perfectly matched). Rather, it is based on how *quickly* they can be brought together. In other words, the objective of lean manufacturing in a job shop or in a custom manufacturing environment is to cut lead time.

Speed to Market

In a mass production system, customer demand is satisfied almost instantaneously because the product already exists. It is sitting in inventory waiting to be sold. When an order is received, all that is required is to pick, pack, and ship. In a job shop, the product must first be produced or even engineered, and this takes lead time, or more accurately customer wait time. Paradoxically, where lean in a mass-production system is based on the idea of operating more like a job shop, lean in a job shop is based on the idea of operating more like a mass-production system—that is, instantaneously.

How Cutting Lead Time Improves Performance and Profitability

As we have seen, a job shop already operates on a pull system, so the focus of lean manufacturing must be on making value flow. Flow is achieved by eliminating delays in the total business process—from the conversion of RFQs to orders, orders to shipments, and accounts receivable to cash. The more quickly customer demand can be satisfied, the more competitive and profitable your company will become. Cutting lead time is a business-development and profit-improvement strategy that will increase sales, reduce costs, improve margins, accelerate cash flow, and increase effective production capacity all at the same time. How?

- ◆ Companies that can bid and ship an order quickly will realize a competitive speed advantage and an increase in sales. The company that can deliver in two weeks has a significant advantage over one that requires a twelve-week lead time.
- ◆ Faster service can command a premium price and produce more winning bids. Our research shows, for example, that getting your bid in front of the buyer before your competitors gives you a huge advantage in getting the order. This is described more fully in Chapter 3.
- ◆ Because custom manufacturers are order-driven, additional sales (order backlog) creates momentum and greater efficiency. When the backlog is down, work has a tendency to get stretched out as

employees want to make the existing work last and management wants to maintain the skill base. There is less pressure to produce when the backlog is low than when it is high.

◆ It is a law of production that the longer an order remains on the shop floor, the more it costs to get it out the door. Orders accumulate costs as they wend their way through a shop. Thus, the less time an order stays on the floor, the less opportunity for costs to add up.

◆ Although some people believe that quality and production are opposites that cannot co-exist, this is not true. A company does not have to sacrifice quality to meet output goals. In fact, the opposite is more often the case. A shop that is operating at a productive pace will generally be able to meet quality goals more consistently than one in which the pace is disjointed, lackadaisical, or chaotic.

◆ The greater the volume of orders through a company, the lower the fixed overhead that must be carried by each order. This creates an opportunity for overall profit improvement and/or improved price competitiveness. More volume comes about as a result of more sales, which is a direct benefit of cutting lead time.

◆ Cash flow is improved. Less working capital is required when the time from quote to cash is compressed (when the time from "money out" to "money in" is shortened, less working capital is required).

The Mother Lode

Whether you call it lean manufacturing, quick-response manufacturing, speed to market, or something else, per-

formance and profit improvement in a custom manufacturing environment boils down to cutting lead time.
When you can deliver quickly, you will not have to shave
prices to get more business. In fact, you can often charge
premium prices for the fast service you provide. When
you can deliver quickly, you can afford to turn down
unprofitable work because you will have plenty of business. The mother lode in a job shop is profitable growth,
not cost savings from inventory reductions. Reducing
lead time is a business-development and profit-improvement strategy, which is not limited to the shop floor.
There is no question that a company that can deliver
quickly will grow and prosper in a just-in-time manufacturing world.

Key Points

◆ The concepts and methods of lean manufacturing
  are derived from mass-production operations,
  therefore, they must be adapted to job shops and
  custom manufacturing environments before they
  can be applied successfully.

◆ The lean strategy of driving out waste by
  minimizing or eliminating inventories does
  not apply in a job shop because there are no
  finished goods inventories to eliminate.

◆ Continuously cutting lead time is essential for
  any make-to-order company wishing to remain
  competitive in a just-in-time world. It is (or
  should be) the objective of lean programs in
  job shop environments.

◆ In a job shop, the mother lode is not cost savings;
  it is the profitable growth that results from cutting
  lead time. A company that can deliver quickly will

grow and prosper in a just-in-time manufacturing world. It is the single most powerful strategy you can follow to strengthen your company's competitive position, improve profits, and secure the future of your business.

◆ Mass-production businesses are focused on getting thinner. Job shops should be focused on getting faster.

References

1. Taiichi Ohno, *The Toyota Production System: Beyond Large-Scale Production*, (Portland, Oregon: Productivity Press, 1998).

2. David Welch, "A Mouse Click, a Car Built: Web May Help Automakers Custom-build Cars in 5 Days," *The Detroit News*, August 15, 1999, Autos section (www.detnews.com/1999/autos/9908/15/index.htm).

N O T E S

NOTES

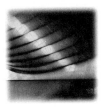

CHAPTER TWO

PROCESS THINKING

Much has been written about the need for managers to think and manage organizational activities in horizontal or process terms. I call this a *process revolution* because it involves a fairly dramatic shift away from hierarchical, pyramid thinking and shows a greater awareness of the need to manage across functional departments and lines. Process thinking enables *horizontal management*, a basic concept that is used for cutting lead time. Process thinking permeates the business world, and is the driving force for changing traditional ideas and methods of management.

Process Defined

A process can be viewed as a horizontal span across an organization. Higher-level, enterprisewide processes cross departmental boundaries and encompass a number of steps or operations. In custom manufacturing, the overall business process generally includes sales, estimating, bidding, order entry, materials management, engineering, production scheduling, production, shipping, and billing (sometimes referred to as "quotes to cash").

This process-based managerial orientation is significantly different from the command-and-control pyramid model where the guiding belief is that you can control the whole by controlling the parts. In this model (which still exists in many companies), functions and departments operate as worlds unto themselves with limited interaction across boundaries. Staff functions do not see themselves as service providers to the operating organization, and as a result have very little value to offer line managers. Decision making is concentrated at the top, and employee involvement is neither expected nor encouraged.

Note: I call this the Humpty-Dumpty theory of organization because it involves breaking a company down into smaller and smaller pieces for the purpose of control (differentiation), while simultaneously trying to put the pieces back together again (integration) so the organization works as a whole. It never does, and people constantly complain about a lack of communication in their companies as a result. This is especially true in larger organizations where greater degrees of differentiation make integration and communication increasingly difficult.

Figure 2-1 illustrates a typical command-and-control organization for a midsize job shop.

Job Shop Business Process

In Chapter 1, cutting lead time was described as a business development strategy that has profitable growth as its objective (the mother lode). However, many companies make the mistake of approaching the challenge of reducing lead time by focusing almost exclusively on manufacturing and ignoring the rest of the organization. But any manufacturing manager will tell you that orders come to the shop late, are inaccurate or illegible, are missing critical information, don't reflect the latest engineering changes, or lack materials, all of which contribute to missing ship dates. A better approach is companywide and takes the entire business process into account.

Figure 2-2 illustrates the flow of activities that make up a typical job shop business process.

When viewed in this way, it is clear that production only comprises one portion of the overall process. The objective, of course, is to compress the time it takes to cycle through all these steps and to serve customers more quickly. That is, to make value flow, which is a key concept in lean manufacturing. Making value flow is accomplished by identifying and eliminating chronological delays throughout the process, but not necessarily by making people work faster.

Note: Processes exist at many levels in organizations. A more detailed view of a job shop business process is provided in Appendix B.

(text continues on page 22)

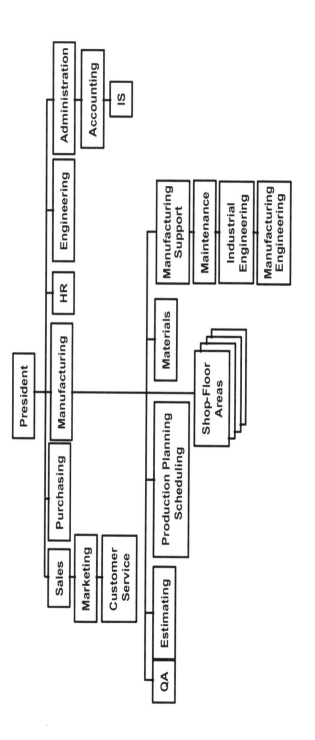

Figure 2-1. A typical job shop organization structure.

Figure 2-2. A job shop business process.

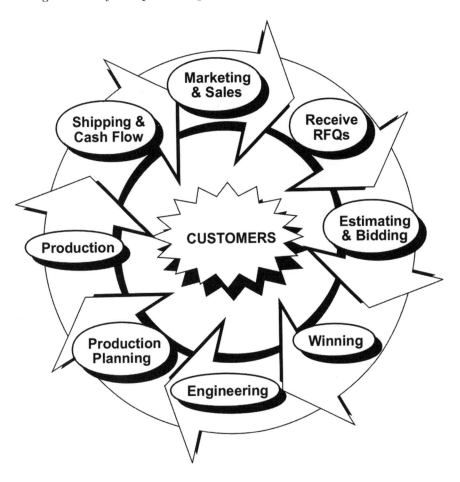

Task Time vs. Chronological Time

To make value flow, you must understand the difference between task time and chronological time. The focus in business has traditionally been on reducing task time, because it is paid for by the hour, and because productivity—more output per hour—has a direct bearing on profitability.

Chronological time, on the other hand, refers to the *process time* required to convert a customer's order through your entire business process from quotes to cash. If you add up all the task time required to convert an RFQ into a quote, for example, it might take only a few hours of work, yet it may take several days to get your quote back to the customer. The objective is to eliminate these days.

The costs of chronological delays in your business are hidden and difficult to measure. Everyone knows what happens to bottom-line profitability when a company reduces labor costs, but it is not obvious how many orders you lost last year because somebody else could deliver to your customers faster. You'll never know, and those lost sales and lost profit dollars will never show up on your income statement.

Eliminating delays that prevent you from serving customers more quickly is the proper focus and objective for any lean manufacturing program in a job shop. When you drive delays out of your total process, your business is guaranteed to grow and prosper.

Note: It is useful to think in terms of *conversion processes* when seeking to improve performance because this keeps the purpose of the process in focus. For example, it is more useful to your organization to focus on the materials acquisition process (purpose) than on purchasing (activities).

Process thinking does not mean hierarchy is eliminated or can be ignored. Process management is not some misguided democratization of the workplace that seeks to put everyone on the same level. Rather, process and structure go together in a manner that is similar to Figure 2-3. If you make the background black and foreground white, you will see two profiles. Conversely, if you see a white background and black foreground, you will see a vase. Process and structure work similarly. They go together.

Good organizational design is based on understanding this relationship. Process constitutes the foundation of the organization. The structure is designed around the process so that it can be managed effectively.

Process Analysis

The technique for identifying and eliminating delays in your business process is called, appropriately enough, *process analysis*. The basic methodology involves making your business process(es) explicit or visible, identifying delays, and systematically eliminating them. *Systematic* is an important keyword because many companies rely on Band-Aid™ fixes as opposed to implementing fundamental structural and systems changes. This is akin to bailing out a leaky boat without patching the holes.

In Chapter 3, process analysis is applied to the first portion of the job shop business process: from sales to winning an order. Process analysis tools are provided in Appendixes C and D.

Figure 2-3. Faces and vases.

Key Points

◆ Viewing your business as a process that converts quotes into cash enables you to organize around and manage the process as opposed to managing activities.

◆ Cutting lead time is not limited to the shop floor. You must take the entire business process into account.

◆ To make value flow, you must understand the difference between task time and chronological time, then eliminate delays.

◆ Lead time is reduced when delays are eliminated.

◆ Process and structure are not conflicting. Good organization design is based on understanding the process, and then designing the structure around it.

◆ Using the modifier *conversion* with the word *process* brings the purpose of a process into view, which is essential for improvement.

◆ You cannot control the whole by controlling the parts.

NOTES

CHAPTER THREE

CUTTING LEAD TIME IN SALES AND ESTIMATING

Eliminating delays from the sales and estimating portion of the job shop business process enables a company to get its quote back to the customer quickly. It is an area for improvement that is often neglected, but which has significant potential for increasing sales.

Turning RFQs around Quickly

Because work is secured through competitive bids in custom manufacturing businesses, estimating the cost of materials, labor, and overhead is a critical function. If the bid is too high, your company may not get the work. If the bid is too low, money will be left on the table and potential profit will be lost. In extreme cases, a too-low bid will not cover all direct and overhead costs.

A typical estimating and bidding process involves the receipt of a request for quotation (RFQ) from a customer, which details product and delivery specifications. (In all likelihood, your company is one of several on the buyer's list that received the same RFQ.) The sales department reviews the RFQ and passes it along to estimating to determine manufacturing and overhead costs. This information is then returned to the sales manager or owner for pricing. Subsequently, the bid—or quote; the terms are used interchangeably—is prepared and sent to the customer.

Figure 3-1 illustrates a typical RFQ to order process.

Figure 3-2 emphasizes the need to eliminate delays throughout your business process, not only on the shop floor. It is based on an analysis of 1,794 RFQs received by one company during the course of a year. The study found more than 50 percent of orders (winning bids) were received within three days of communicating the bid to the customer.

What Does This Mean?

Normally, we think of the quoting process as one in which a customer prepares specifications and sends these to three or more potential suppliers in the form of an RFQ. These suppliers prepare estimates that are converted into bids or quotes by the sales department, and sent back to the customer. The customer waits to receive the quotes, compares them, and then makes a rational decision based on price, delivery, and quality factors.

It doesn't always work in this ideal way, however. Many times customers have an urgent need—somebody

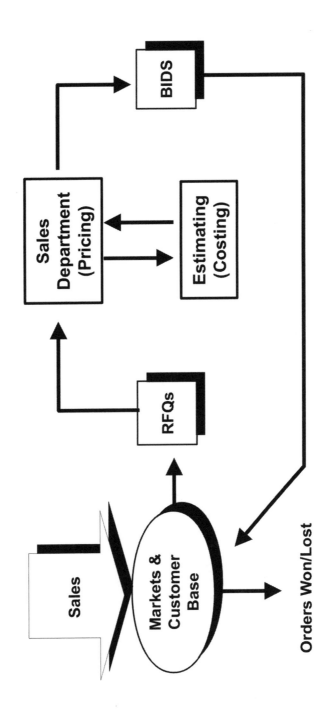

Figure 3-1. A typical RFQ to order process.

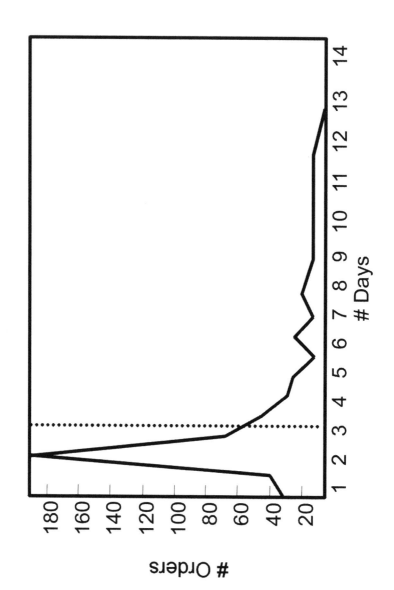

Figure 3-2. The time from quote to order.

forgot to order the parts, or a previous shipment was unusable, or their inventory records were inaccurate, or one of their customers pushed a delivery date forward. Whatever the reason, customers have an urgent need for what you supply and the normal bidding process is bypassed.

In these cases (50 percent of the time according to this and other studies), getting your quote in front of the buyer before your competitors gives you a huge sales advantage because the most important thing for that customer is to get what he or she needs as soon as possible. Do you think the customer is going to sit and wait for all the bids to dribble in possibly to save a few dollars when he or she is dealing with an urgent problem? Hardly! There is no question that the company that can convert an RFQ into a bid (and an order into a shipment) in the least amount of time will realize a valuable advantage over its competitors.

Note: When RFQs are issued, buyers typically have a delivery date in mind or specified. The clock starts running when the RFQ is issued, not when the order is won. Often, lost time in estimating and quoting must be made up later on the shop floor. This can become very expensive, especially when you have to expedite production to meet a promised ship date by rescheduling orders in the queue, working overtime, or stopping work on other orders.

Process Analysis Applied

When the RFQ-to-order process is examined in detail, it becomes clear that delays can result in several of the following steps:

1. In receiving information from the customer
2. In preparing the estimate
3. In bid pricing
4. In bid preparation and communication back to the customer
5. In process-step delays, which represent the "transfer," or communication, time from one step to another within your company

Receiving Information from the Customer

Many times customers do not provide all the information estimating requires. They may fail to include accurate prints, tolerances, materials specifications, order quantities, special packing and shipping requirements, or delivery dates. When critical information that must be obtained from the customer is lacking from the RFQ, delays enter into the process.

This problem can be further aggravated when estimators are not allowed to have direct customer contact. Sometimes this is motivated by the fear that the estimator and the customer will get too cozy, and somehow this relationship will be detrimental to the business. I would argue exactly the opposite: Your estimators should have well-developed working relationships with the technical people in your customers' organizations.

Look at it this way, estimators in job shops must have a high degree of knowledge about how the shop works and alternative ways of producing things. If your estimators can find better ways to meet your customers' needs through direct dialogue, this will forge better links with those customers. You will get more of their business because you provide greater value than your competitors (and are probably easier to work with as well). Many companies have a policy limiting who can communicate directly with customers. If yours is one of these companies, you might do well to revisit the logic behind your policies.

In companies where direct communication is restricted, the request for information must be relayed internally to the designated customer-contact person in the organization, usually someone in sales, who must then communicate with his or her counterpart in the customer's organization, who then has to go to his or her technical people to get the answer—and on it goes, adding delay after delay into the process. Figure 3-3 illustrates these types of time-consuming, inefficient communications routines.

Actions You Can Take

◆ *Review your customer-contact policy.* You may be better off allowing estimators to talk to technical people in the customer's organization rather than funneling communications through your organization, which creates additional delays. Building these types of cooperative working relationships with your customers can go a long way toward developing loyalty and repeat business. This is an example of a fundamental system modification as opposed to a Band-Aid™ fix as mentioned previously. (A Band-Aid™ fix would be to allow your estimator to have direct contact for a specific order; a systemic fix would be to modify your customer-contact policy.)

◆ *Institute a standard data collection form.* Although it would be nice to train your regular customers to

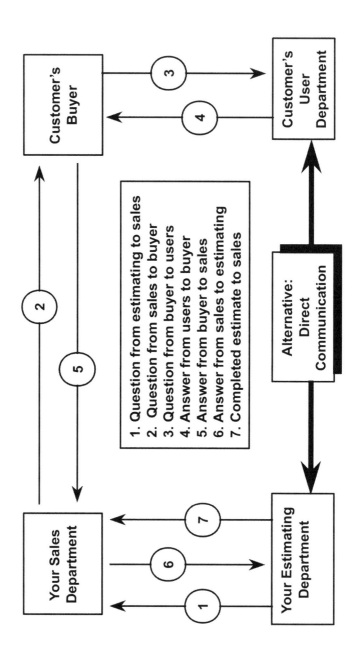

Figure 3-3. A comparison of direct and indirect communications between customers and suppliers.

provide information in the form that your esti-mators (and costing system) require, it may not be practical. However, consider instituting a standard data-collection form or computer screen for entering information from customers' RFQs. Review this information with estimating imme-diately. If data are lacking, contact the customer right away. This will eliminate some of the delays in the process, giving your estimators the infor-mation they require.

◆ *Separate standard bids from bids requiring special treat-ment.* Establishing a two-track bidding process often makes sense and will expedite both types of bids.

Note: Some companies have instituted a fast-track process for urgent orders. These orders are separated from the normal production process, receive special treatment, and are priced at a premium. Establishing this level of service also enables you to minimize requests for faster service that are not really necessary (for example, bogus "rush" orders). It is not uncommon for customers to second-guess your lead times and delivery reliability by requesting a shorter than needed lead time. However, when they have to pay more for it, they will be less inclined to play this game.

Preparing the Estimate

Preparing estimates can take longer than necessary when estimators are required to go through a lengthy, compli-cated process to get the information they need. Time can be saved and accuracy improved when standard costs, routings, materials costs, overhead rates, and similar information are properly organized, current, accurate, and easily accessible. Also, it is important to ensure that estimating is aware of engineering and production changes that affect costs.

Delays result when estimating is required to revise estimates after the fact. An important question to ask is: Are estimators using the latest engineering changes and production information, or are they working from old cost and routing information that is obsolete?

Actions You Can Take

◆ *Review the estimating process with everyone involved.* Identify typical delays and brainstorm ways to eliminate them. (Note: When you involve people in identifying problems and proposing solutions, make certain that you follow through and implement the changes.)

◆ *Train another person to handle less complex estimates during peak workload periods.* Adding capacity will reduce the backlog of RFQs and associated delays during peak periods.

◆ *Automate the estimating process.* There are a number of software programs on the market that can facilitate estimating. The computer does not replace the need for human thought, interpretation, and judgment. Rather, it automates routine portions of the task so that greater attention can be focused on the more important aspects.

◆ *Set a reasonable time expectation for preparing estimates, and measure performance against this goal.*

Bid Pricing

Who sets the price? When a cost estimate is completed, the bid submitted to the customer must be increased to include the profit margin. This is certainly not an exact science and depends upon a wide range of variables. Delays enter into the process when too many people get involved in pricing decisions, or when responsibility is unclear, or when the person responsible for the final sign-off (often the owner) is unavailable. How the price is determined and who sets it is an important area to include in any shop's business-process review.

Actions You Can Take

◆ Review the process for making pricing decisions in your company.
◆ Streamline the process.
◆ Eliminate obvious bottlenecks, delays, and communication gaps.
◆ Clarify responsibilities and pricing policies.

Bid Preparation and Communication to the Customer

Once the estimate and pricing have been completed, the next step is to prepare a formal bid to send to the customer. This may be as simple as a letter or standard form, or it may be a more elaborate package. You can lose valuable response time when the task of preparing and communicating the bid is delayed. This can happen for a variety of reasons, most of which tend to be administrative.

Actions You Can Take

Review the process for preparing formal bid documents, and make certain that:

◆ There is backup for the person responsible for preparing bids to cover for absences, vacations, or workload demands.

◆ Priorities are clear; that is, bids are completed and sent before other routine administrative tasks.

◆ The bid is not more elaborate or complex than it needs to be.

◆ The transfer of information to the person who actually prepares and sends the bid is complete, accurate, and not delayed by the sales department.

◆ The methods used to physically send the bid to the customer must be reviewed. Some companies find it advantageous to fax or e-mail bids and then send hard copy by regular mail. Overnight delivery is another option.

Process Step Delays

This refers to the transfer time between steps as the RFQ moves through your organizational process. This can add up to a significant amount of lost days depending upon the number of steps and people involved.

Actions You Can Take

◆ When reviewing the total process for converting RFQs to bids, make certain that completed work is passed along immediately. Also, ensure that everyone involved understands the importance of a quick response, has a sense of urgency, and works together to get your bid in the customer's hands as quickly as possible.

◆ Set a reasonable time expectation for converting RFQs to bids, measure performance against this goal, and provide feedback to the organization members who are involved.

Note: What is a good hit rate? What percentage of the quotes you submit should you expect to win? You can figure that if buyers in your industry typically send out three RFQs to prospective vendors, then the law of averages would suggest you should win one out of three or 33 percent if all things are relatively equal—such as price, quality, and delivery time. If you are winning fewer than a third, it would be worthwhile to find out why since your price may be too high, delivery time too long, or reliability inconsistent.

On the other hand, if you are winning more than your fair share, your pricing may be too low. Also, recognize you may be competing against four or five other shops not two, so the law of averages would result in a lower percentage of wins. You may also find it valuable to measure dollars bid versus dollars won as well as absolute numbers of wins.

Marketing and Sales

It is one thing to improve your company's ability to respond quickly to customers' RFQs and quite another to get the RFQs to come in the door in the first place. Because custom manufacturers and job shops are generally known within an industry, they tend to be automatically included on supplier lists when RFQs are issued. As a result, marketing and lead generation may be taken for granted. Increases and decreases in sales volume that rise and fall with the fortunes of the industry may also be accepted. It is not uncommon for all of a company's business to come from a handful of customers. In some instances, a company is completely dependent upon a single account. This, of course, makes the company vulnerable to industry fluctuations and overly dependent upon specific customers. When a major account is lost, the company may not be able to recover.

The reduction of lead time can be used as a growth strategy because faster service will generally enable your company to win more bids without sacrificing price. However, an equally important focus is on generating a greater number of RFQs, which represents more opportunities to bid on and win work. This requires either investing in new technologies, machinery, equipment, or facilities that will enable you to provide improved, different, or a greater variety of services to your current customer base; or it requires attracting more customers you can serve with your existing capabilities, expertise, and equipment.

The best time to seek new business is when business is good. Don't wait for a downturn or disaster to strike. Even the best customers move on, get lost, or fall out of favor, so the need to replenish a company's customer base is a constant and ongoing requirement. This can be accomplished in a number of ways:

Identifying and Targeting Additional Industries

This requires a bit of research to determine additional high-opportunity industries that fit a shop's production technology and capabilities. For example, one of our clients expanded its business significantly by identifying and targeting poultry and fish processing as a market for its machine parts. This required the company to learn how to process new types of steel, establish additional sources of supply for these materials, and establish a presence in the food-processing industry. The sales, margin results, and stability have been well worth the effort.

Advertising and Promotion

There are many ways to make potential customers aware of your company and its capabilities. For starters, consider:

◆ Conducting a direct mail program
◆ Using telemarketing
◆ Hiring a salesperson or expanding the sales force/rep organization
◆ Placing an advertisement in the *Thomas Register*
◆ Establishing a Web site on the Internet
◆ Airport advertising
◆ Attending new and different trade shows
◆ Advertising in trade and industry publications
◆ Sponsoring seminars and workshops
◆ Being creative . . .

Key Points

◆ Turning RFQs around quickly will increase the likelihood of winning an order, especially when a buyer is under pressure to solve a problem.
◆ Lost time in estimating and quoting can increase costs, especially when you have to expedite production to meet promised ship dates.
◆ Cutting lead time in estimating and bidding requires a step-by-step review of your process in order to identify and eliminate delays.
◆ In addition to responding quickly to RFQs, profitable growth also requires generating more opportunities to bid.

NOTES

CHAPTER FOUR

CUTTING LEAD TIME IN PREPRODUCTION AREAS

Preproduction is defined as that portion of the business process from order entry to the start of production on the floor. Preproduction activities typically include order entry, production planning and scheduling, engineering, purchasing, and materials management. There are many opportunities for reducing delays and lost time in these areas. The failure to organize and manage this portion of the process can be a major factor in missing ship dates, increasing costs, eroding profitability, and undermining customer service.

This is a more complex part of the process compared to estimating and quoting, which was described in Chapter 3. More people and functions are involved, including outside vendors, and this requires greater coordination and communication. Consequently, there are more opportunities for mistakes, missed dates, and delays to occur.

Order Entry

The receipt of an order initiates a series of preproduction activities that must be completed before the order can be released to the floor. When an order is received, it is sound practice to ensure that all the information necessary for production is included, and that the specified ship date can be met. At a minimum, this requires communication with production planning, engineering, purchasing, and materials management. It may also require coordination with manufacturing, engineering, quality assurance, production, and industrial engineering, as well as outside vendors. Delays resulting from orders that are not checked for accuracy and completeness will not show up immediately in order entry *per se*, but will cause lost time when they surface further downstream in the process on the floor.

Once it is determined that a ship date can be met, a confirmation is normally returned to the customer. In cases where a specified ship date cannot be met—for example, lack of materials with long lead times, extensive engineering work required, or load on the shop—communication with the customer is required to establish a new, more realistic date.

Some shops omit this step for fear of losing the order

and will let the customer believe their order will be shipped on time when this is not possible. Later, when the customer starts screaming for his or her parts, the shop goes through all kinds of contortions to get the shipment out the door. This creates unnecessary disruptions, causes the rescheduling of other orders in production, adds unnecessary costs, angers the customer, delays other customers' shipments, creates ill will, and damages a company's reputation for reliability. This is a high price to pay for the risk of losing an occasional order.

Note: Many customers now require bidders to provide an accurate delivery date as part of their quote. This means that coordination among preproduction functions must occur during the estimating and bidding stage of the process to ensure factors such as the availability of raw materials, delivery of tooling and purchased parts, or existence of engineering drawings. This legwork can save a great deal of time when an order is received. However, in those cases where a bid is not won and no order is forthcoming, this work will go without reward and adds to the general cost of doing business. This requirement illustrates the increasing importance customers are placing on delivery dates and reliability.

Delays in Order Entry

Time can be lost when orders are not entered into your system immediately, but are allowed to stack up for batch processing. This practice is usually established as an administrative convenience for the benefit of clerical personnel. However, it can cost a shop critical production days when new orders are not processed quickly. At the very least, new orders should be checked and entered on the day they are received, if not immediately upon receipt.

Another source of delay results from cumbersome and time-consuming credit checks for new customers. One problem involves delays in receiving information from external sources, such as banks, Dun & Bradstreet, or trade accounts. Daily follow-up is the key to getting this information when responses are not received promptly. Sometimes, office staff are reluctant to do this for a variety of reasons—they may feel they are "bothering someone" or they don't fully understand that time lost here costs expensive production time later—so it is important to review policies and procedures in this area, and retrain people as required.

Actions You Can Take

Make certain that your processes are not overly cumbersome, information requests are precise (for example, avoid requesting information with little or no practical value), paperwork is kept to a minimum, delays are eliminated, and everyone understands the importance of getting new orders into the system as quickly as possible. It should be noted that, from a customer's point of view, the clock starts running when the RFQ is issued or the order is placed, not when it is released to the shop for production.

Production Planning, Engineering, Materials Management, and Purchasing

There are wide variations among shops in terms of responsibilities and activities performed by these functions. Variations result from differences in a company's size, products, production technology, customers' requirements, inventory policy, organization structure, and even employees' capabilities and leadership strengths. Consequently, your shop may be organized differently from this description.

Although preproduction functions are generally separate organizationally, in practical terms, they must work together to ensure that an order can be completed and shipped on time. In most cases it doesn't make sense to release an order to the floor when tooling is not available, or routings are being revised, or materials are not available since this will cause start-and-stop production, increase work-in-process (WIP), add costs, consume cash, and generally prevent the shop from functioning more efficiently.

Note: This is a good example of the Humpty-Dumpty theory of organization mentioned previously. Production planning, materials management, engineering, purchasing, manufacturing engineering, quality assurance, industrial engineering, and other preproduction functions are generally separated and lack integration. Consider using the concept of *preproduction* to organize these functions into one unit.

Typically, orders are arranged by ship dates and back-scheduled through the various production steps to determine release dates to the floor. When a release date is missed, production time is shortened because the ship date is considered to be a fixed commitment. In effect, delays in preproduction eat up shop time and contribute to late shipments. Therefore, it is as important to measure on-time performance from preproduction as it is to measure on-time delivery to customers. If an order is not released to the shop on time, the likelihood of missing the ship date increases.

Note: Many companies only measure on-time delivery to customers. Consider tracking orders released to the shop late and compare these to on-time delivery. If the percentage of orders released late is greater than late shipments, you will know whether the shop is compensating for delays in other parts of your process. This will help you to recognize those areas that are underperforming so you can take appropriate corrective actions. Table 4-1 illustrates this concept:

Table 4-1. Released late vs. shipped late reasons for delay.

Orders	Released to Shop	Shipped to Customers
% On-Time	60%	80%
% Late	40%	20%

Organization of Preproduction Functions

Figure 4-1 illustrates the relationships among production planning, scheduling, engineering, and materials management, which is typically a function of purchasing in smaller shops. In this model, overall coordination falls to production planning (via the master schedule), which is responsible for release dates and shop schedules.

A Note on Master Scheduling

The master schedule is often a misunderstood and poorly used tool. It represents an overall organizational planning and coordinating mechanism that enables management to meet customer demand with the most efficient

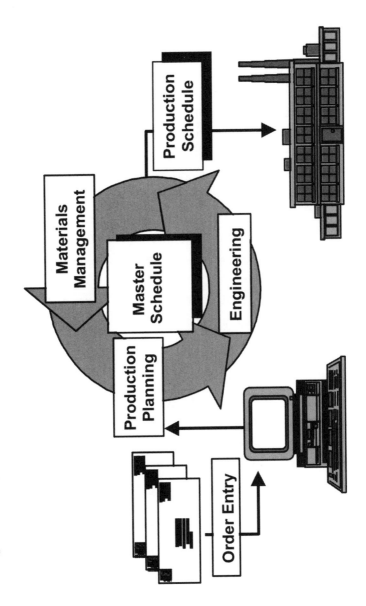

Figure 4-1. Organization of preproduction functions.

use of a company's resources. It is the *plan* for what is to be built during the time horizon the master schedule covers.

Properly used, master scheduling coordinates capacity, customer commitments, production schedules, and purchased materials or components. It can also include non-manufacturing areas (for example, engineering, tooling, testing, or materials) when they are critical in determining schedules. One of its many benefits is to bring about greater control over lead time and to improve on-time ship performance to meet customer commitments.

The tendency in many companies is to overshedule, that is, to make the schedule too heavy for the capacity of the plant. This occurs because the schedule is misperceived as a tool for increasing productivity, which it is not, and this confusion inevitably leads to unrealistic production schedules that cannot be met. This, in turn, creates unnecessary delays and increases costs.

Further, overscheduling leads to a loss of confidence and credibility in order-completion dates. The result is that informal controls come into use (for example, hot lists or super hot lists), along with a great deal of confusing and expensive expediting. Therefore, it is essential that the master schedule be realistically related to production capacities and lead times in order to gain a greater degree of manufacturing predictability and control.

When sales demand or production problems require a change in plan, master scheduling informs management of the anticipated consequences. The advantage is that management will know before the fact rather than after, and can decide on some combination of solution alternatives—for example, to authorize overtime, use alternative resources, or revise delivery dates.

This early warning system enables anticipatory problem solving. In effect, the more accurate and usable the master schedule, the sooner you will know of potential problems and delays in the production process. Knowing about problems sooner rather than later increases the range of less costly solution options available to you. The more often your management team can carry out anticipatory problem solving, the fewer fires you'll have to put out. Once an alternative is selected, the schedule is updated to reflect that decision.

Purchasing and Materials Management

Some people are under the mistaken impression you cannot forecast materials requirements in a job shop environment. However, one key for reducing lead time in job shops and custom manufacturing is to have sufficient raw materials in inventory, or readily available, to meet most production requirements. If your shop has to wait to receive materials from its suppliers—for example, you order materials after receiving an order from a customer—this practice will reduce your ability to service that customer quickly. Linked lead-time dependency means that your lead time is dependent upon suppliers' lead times and reliability in meeting promised ship dates. This can be disastrous for your business when your vendors are unreliable or when it takes a long time to get materials.

This may not be a problem, however. It depends upon the type of material used and the number of materials suppliers in your area. For example, one of our clients uses specialty steels imported from Germany. Because long lead times are involved, they must forecast their demand accurately and manage this inventory closely. However, for other products where they use common steels, these are readily available from local distributors on short notice, so accurately forecasting and maintaining these inventories is less critical.

Note: A secondary problem in this area bears mention. A shop may substitute available materials that exceed a customer's specifications in order to fill an order quickly. For example, a thicker gauge or higher quality steel may be used because it is on hand. Not only does this increase the basic materials costs over and above the estimate, which is a source of profit erosion, it may also require additional work and cost on the shop floor to remove more excess material (for example, forming, shaping, or grinding). In these cases, a blanket policy to reduce inventories, which is considered Holy Writ in many companies, is really a false economy that should be examined and modified as required.

Any decision regarding the mix and quantities of raw materials to inventory must balance the cost to carry this inventory versus the value of being able to fill orders quickly. Additional factors to consider when making this decision would include, for example, the value of increased sales, avoidance of lost sales, production inefficiencies, or increased cost of using substitute materials. When additional sales and profitable growth are dependent upon short lead times, the management of raw materials inventories becomes a critical competitive factor.

Engineering

There is a wide range of engineering capabilities among shops, which can extend from basic activities, such as drawing prints and preparing specifications and routers for production, to prototype design and testing, sometimes with limited production runs.

In some cases engineering is essential to sales. For example, one of our clients (a manufacturer of electrical devices) would routinely design products to solve customers' problems with the hope that customers would order these products in sufficient volume to cover engineering costs. Upon analysis, this turned out not to be the case and a new policy to charge modestly for these services was implemented. This had the side benefit of reducing the number of frivolous requests from customers as well as covering the basic cost of this service. Generally speaking, the more extensive and sophisticated the engineering activities, the more difficult it is to manage and integrate this function into the overall order conversion process.

Sources of Delays in Engineering

Engineering is often a source of delay in the process of converting an order into a shipment, and a great deal of time can be lost in this area. Typically, this is due to a number of factors:

◆ *The nature of the work itself.* As much as we may think of engineering as a logical and precise discipline, trial and error is involved since concepts and designs on paper don't always work as intended in physical reality. "Going back to the drawing board" is a common phrase and truism in engineering work. Often, it is difficult to estimate how much engineering time will really be required, especially when new products and designs are involved. However, this is often used as an excuse for delays, so it is important to review work-estimating methods and scheduling procedures.

♦ *The tendency toward perfection.* There are few designs that cannot be improved, and engineers who take pride in their work will naturally strive for the optimum. "Good enough" may not be good enough when professional pride is involved, and much time can be consumed in finessing designs that are already fit for use.

♦ *The fluctuating workload.* Workload variations can create backlogs in engineering exactly as they do on the shop floor. It may make sense to subcontract or outsource engineering work during these periods. This is generally a less expensive way to add more capacity than hiring permanent engineering staff. As the old adage goes, "You don't build the church for Easter Sunday" . . . or staff your engineering department for peak workloads if you want to maintain profitability.

♦ *Engineering priorities are not customer or company priorities.* Engineers, like everyone else, like to work on projects that are interesting and challenging to them, and so tend to set their own priorities. Less interesting work may be put on the back burner, even though these projects may have a higher overall company or customer priority. Engineering can become disconnected from the overall business process when there is no coordinating mechanism for establishing and aligning engineering's priorities with the overall needs of the business and its customers. (One of our clients referred to its engineering department as "the black hole"—work went in but didn't come out.)

◆ *Lack of an effective project management and scheduling system.* The workload in any engineering department must be managed in an orderly and disciplined fashion. Priorities must be set, project completion dates taken seriously, on-time performance tracked, and accountability demanded. Often, project management and scheduling systems are lacking, or if they do exist, are not used. Extensive delays can enter into the overall order-to-ship process when engineering is disconnected from the business and operates as a world unto itself.

Note: Some companies have found it advantageous to establish engineering as an "internal vendor," which operates as a separate profit center on a fee-for-service basis. Engineering is held to the same standards of cost and service as other external service vendors, and may compete with them.

Summary of Actions You Can Take to Reduce Delays in Preproduction Areas

◆ Ensure that order-entry routines are streamlined, orders are entered promptly, credit checks are expedited, and everyone has a sense of urgency and understands the need to get orders entered into the system ASAP. Retrain staff as required.

◆ Review master scheduling concepts and methods. Ensure that capacity is not overscheduled, and that all areas that have an impact on the production schedule are represented and coordinated.

◆ Review materials inventories policies, especially blanket "reduce inventories" directives. Analyze and compare the cost-to-carry inventory versus the benefits of reduced lead times. Determine appropriate inventory investment and materials mix.

◆ Establish policies and procedures that support a short lead-time/quick-response strategy. Forecast critical materials requirements and manage inventories closely, especially where long lead-time items are involved.

◆ Analyze your suppliers' on-time delivery performance, quality, and reliability. Seek out new sources of supply when supplier performance is found wanting.

◆ Review typical factors that cause engineering delays and establish new policies and procedures as required. Ensure that the engineering department is managed with a practical project management system.

◆ Establish a system to ensure that engineering's priorities are aligned with your company's strategy and customer service objectives.

◆ Consider outsourcing engineering work when workload fluctuations cause backlogs and delays.

◆ Measure the engineering department's performance in terms of on-time project completion and project costs and demand accountability.

◆ Organizationally, ensure that preproduction functions are logically integrated and work together effectively. Consider organizing preproduction functions in one group with the appropriate leadership.

◆ Establish an "exceptions only" policy to ensure that orders are not routinely released to the floor when they cannot be completed.

Key Points

◆ When orders released to the floor are late or incomplete, valuable production time is lost and costs increase.

◆ Significant improvements in lead time can be achieved when unnecessary delays in order entry, engineering, and materials management are identified and eliminated.

◆ Delays in preproduction lead to a deterioration of on-time delivery performance and customer service. If left uncorrected over time, the practice of missing promised ship dates will have a damaging effect on your business and undermine its future.

◆ Measure on-time order release to the floor exactly as you measure on-time ship performance.

◆ *Preproduction* can be a useful concept for organizing and managing this portion of your business process.

◆ Carrying inventory is not always bad, especially when additional sales and profitable growth are dependent upon short lead times.

N O T E S

CHAPTER FIVE

THE SHOP FLOOR

In this chapter, the emphasis moves to the next portion of the process: the shop floor. Because manufacturing operations are so diverse and so much has been written in the last few years about how to improve them, the objective here is to concentrate on a few key areas, and illustrate them with real-life examples from companies that have been successful using various concepts and techniques.

One of the most important steps you can take to position your company for profitable growth is to ensure your business is properly aligned with its markets and customers. Although this issue falls into the realm of organization design and applies to the total business process, misalignments will show up on the shop floor as unnecessary delays, poor customer service, a lack of control, and inefficiencies in production.

Recognizing Two Businesses under the Same Roof

It is not uncommon to find shops that make to order also produce a standard line of products they build to stock. Problems arise when these divisions compete for common manufacturing capacity, and are not recognized and organized as separate business or value streams with different requirements. Build-to-stock and build-to-order businesses operate on completely different models, as discussed in Chapter 1, but can get muddled together when they share common manufacturing processes. When fundamental differences between them are not recognized and managed appropriately, both can suffer.

Case Example

One of our clients manufactures a variety of hand tools that are sold to professional tradesmen and do-it-yourselfers through home centers, hardware stores, and professional supply houses. This is a build-to-stock business. Orders are filled from finished goods inventories, which are replenished through a materials requirements planning (MRP) system. The company also manufactures machine blades to meet original equipment manufacturers' specifications. This is a made-to-order business where sales are secured through a bidding process in response to RFQs.

Management had been frustrated with the performance of the machine-blade area for many years and tried different improvement programs with little or no success. The primary problem quickly became apparent during our assessment—the manufacture of machine blades was regarded as a department, not a separate business with its own customer base and manufacturing technology. Fundamental business differences between tools and blades were not being recognized and managed. The organization structure did not distinguish between the two businesses and managerial responsibilities were unclear.

Since these differences—and their managerial implications—were not well-recognized within the larger organization, it was essential to clarify them. This was done with a *differentiation matrix*, a tool that is used for comparing and contrasting critical business characteristics. Everyone involved had an opportunity to provide his or her input regarding what he or she perceived to be important differences. Forty-two specifics were identified regarding product characteristics, materials, sales and marketing, human resources, manufacturing, and general business attributes. Once these differences were clearly portrayed, the path was clear for rethinking and redesigning the business and supporting organization.

Figure 5-1 illustrates how this business was reconceptualized, and provides another view of the differences between a mass production system and a job shop. Both businesses make products from flat sheet steel, and share a common portion of their manufacturing processes. Forming is accomplished by using dies and laser cutting. Manufacturing starts with a customer order (real demand) in the job shop division and a materials requirements

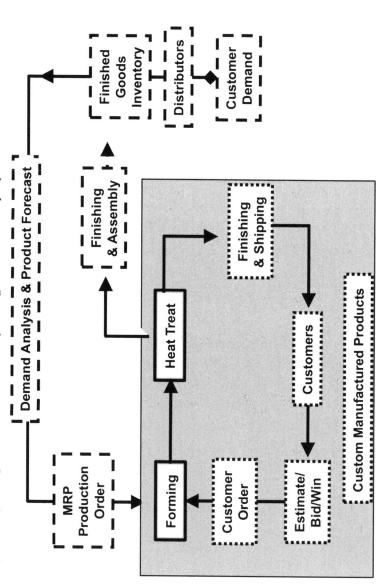

Figure 5-1. Job shop and build-to-stock manufacturing in the same company.

planning order (anticipated sales demand for some future period) in the mass-production division.

Organizing by Type of Demand

Along these same lines, many shops fail to differentiate among types of orders. However, understanding differences can often enable a shop to operate more efficiently and effectively as the following example illustrates.

Note: The term *value stream* is a good concept for identifying differences in types of demand served by a company. These can be recognized as subconversion processes within the overall business process, and may involve differences in production technology, customer types, products, and other variables. For example, some shops have a large volume of repeat orders with customers who demand short lead times. It would probably make good business sense to handle this value stream differently from first-time orders. In effect, the repetitive order value stream can be regarded as a separate business with its own set of requirements and processes.

In other cases, it may be appropriate to differentiate between customers who require extensive quality documentation and those who do not, or to separate build-to-stock from build-to-order. Differentiating among value streams, making them explicit, and organizing around them provides management with a more focused, streamlined organization that is better aligned with its markets and customers, thereby making the company easier to manage and generally more profitable.

Case Example

One of our clients is a job shop that makes hydraulic valves and related devices, which are sold to a variety of OEMs (original equipment manufacturers) customers and contractors. The $10-million business has been growing steadily, doubling in the last three years. The company's manufacturing process includes machining, honing, assembly, and testing operations.

This company was able to benefit significantly from viewing their business horizontally, differentiating among sources of demand (value streams), and organizing accordingly. Figure 5-2 illustrates the company's situation.

♦ The majority of demand (approximately 75 percent) comes from high-volume original equipment manufacturers who use hydraulic components in their materials handling equipment. These manufacturers supply the shop with demand forecasts and follow-up with firm production schedules well in advance of their needs. This is essentially a just-in-time (JIT) business with no finished goods inventories.

♦ A second source of demand is unpredictable and very short term (i.e., "We need it yesterday."). This demand stream must be managed differently from the JIT business, and includes forecasting anticipated requirements, analyzing anticipated demand for the most common components, and building component inventory to cover the majority of these requirements. When an order is received, components are selected from inventory, assembled, tested, and shipped. If the shop had to build components from scratch, lead times would be

Figure 5-2. A job shop organized by type of demand.

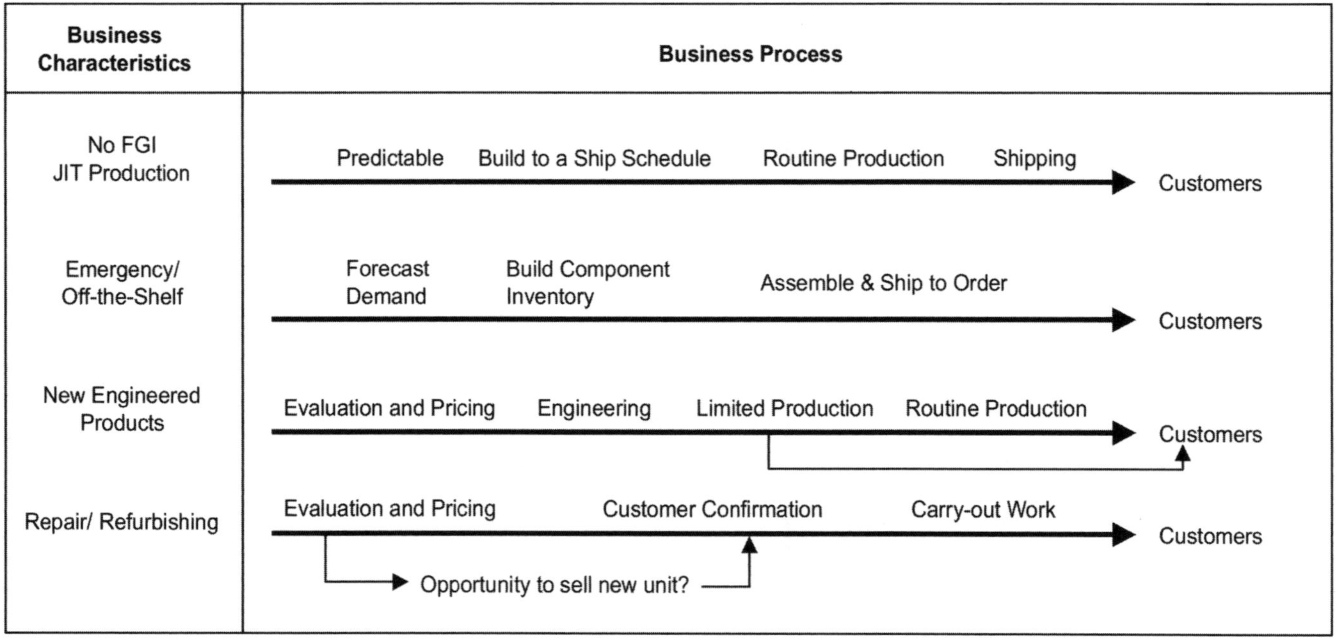

much longer and normal production would be disrupted unnecessarily.

◆ A third source of demand is for custom applications that must be engineered. This is a different process because it usually requires prototypes to be built, which may then lead to full-scale production. Engineering costs are also involved, which may be priced separately.

◆ The company also has a repair business that is growing along with its volume. This involves replacing seals, honing bores, and recalibrating settings. Machining or replacing major components is generally not required. Repair is an entirely different process that must be managed as well.

Recognizing the differences among types of demand, and understanding how to manage them, provided this company with a solid organizing concept and foundation to support their continuing growth.

Many job shops supply markets through multiple value streams. It is important to differentiate clearly among them and to manage them according to their so-called natures.

Reducing Setup Time

One of the most important areas to address is reducing setup or changeover of machines and equipment from one job to another. One technique that has been used successfully by many companies is to videotape and analyze an actual changeover as it happens on the floor. The method is relatively straightforward: Set up a video camera to focus on the piece of equipment, make certain the elapsed time recording feature is turned on, and video-tape the entire process starting from the last piece of the previous run to the first good piece produced on the new run. This is the total changeover time.

Next, get everyone who has a role in changeovers involved—operators, setup people, supervisors, production-scheduling staff, and manufacturing engineers—to review the videotape and critique the process. Typically, you will find time periods when nothing is happening and no one is working on the equipment. This is called recoverable lost time, and represents improvement potential. This can be as much as half or more of the total elapsed changeover time.

It is helpful to have someone who is not directly involved facilitate this review. Record periods when no one is working directly on the equipment. Find out what is going on during these off-task periods. For example, you may find that changeover activity does not start immediately and the machine sits idle after the last piece of the run is produced. Or you may find that activity stops because a wrench or special tool is missing. Or that dies or tooling must be retrieved from the tool room, rather than being staged at the machine beforehand. Or that the changeover occurs during break time. Or that material is not staged for the next run. Or that the regular setup person is unavailable, so people are fumbling around trying to figure out what to do.

Note: You will also be able to note excessive time requirements when tasks are actually being performed on the piece of equipment—for example, the wrong tool is being used, or bolts are too long, or tasks are out of sequence, or it takes too long to change dies. These types of conditions also represent opportunities for improvement and should be addressed.

Once the videotape review is completed and off-task time and reasons are documented, the next step is to set the goal (for example, eliminate all off-task or idle time), brainstorm corrective actions, and develop a more efficient, planned process. Document the new process, implement organizational and procedural changes, and train people as required. *Effective planning and preparation is the key to improvement.* Retape at a future date to ensure changes have been implemented, and the goal has been achieved. This will also enable you to identify opportunities for further reductions.

Process-Step Value Analysis

This is a useful technique for achieving quick results in any lead-time reduction program and improving overall shop-floor performance. The basic idea is to look at everything that happens to an order as it actually progresses through the shop. The objective is to identify those activities that add value and those that do not, so that non-value-adding activities can be eliminated. *Value adding* can be defined as anything that changes the physical form of the product.

The technique itself is straightforward. A team is organized to follow the progress of an order through the sequence of operations on the floor. One person writes every activity that is performed on a task/activity analysis worksheet, and another team member counts the walking steps from one operation to another to determine travel distances. Another notes the typical transfer time from one operation to the next. The team as a whole makes collective decisions as to whether or not a particular task or activity adds value from the customer's point of view, which can usually be easily determined. No changes or decisions are made at this time since this is only a fact-finding process at this stage.

Once the walk-through has been completed, the team analyzes every step using a process critique guide. The objective is to eliminate or combine operations or tasks, determine changes in methods or tools, reduce distances traveled, eliminate delays from one operation to the next, and generally look for ways to move the work through the manufacturing process more expeditiously. Table 5-1 summarizes the results of a process-step value analysis performed by one company.

Table 5-1. Results of a process-step value analysis.

Process	Steps Before	After	To Eliminate
Value-Adding Activities	14	12	2
Moves	17	6	11
Wait/Store/File	16	0	16
Log, Weigh, Count	5	0	5
Clean, Scrape, Bundle	9	4	5
Requisition, Order	2	0	2
Other	1	0	1
Total Activities	**64**	**22**	**42**
Distance Traveled (Ft.)	**7,107**	**2,151**	**4,956**

Note: Once these decisions have been confirmed, the next step is to implement the team's recommendations. This is where many programs falter because management is often reluctant to make other than token changes. However, significant opportunities for improvement often require drastic measures, such as moving machines to better suit the process flow. Once employees see these types of changes occurring, they know that management is serious about improvement and will participate meaningfully in the process. (See Appendix D, "How to Conduct a Process-Step Value Analysis," for a complete description of this technique.)

Revising Overdetermined Quality Programs

The great push for quality in U.S. industry has created numerous examples of companies that are put at a disadvantage by overdetermined quality programs. That is, quality programs that are so excessive and demanding in their requirements that they amount to overkill. Often, these programs are mandated by large customers so if a supplier does not comply, he or she will essentially be out of business.

♦ *A major problem with many programs is poor design.* Since much of the current quality-improvement technology originated in high-volume, mass-production manufacturing, it may not fit job shops and make-to-order environments. Statistical process control (SPC) is a good example of a tool that can be useful in mass production, but misapplied in a job shop environment.

♦ *Another major problem is data overload.* The tendency of many quality programs is to measure too much of everything, which generates so much data that it cannot be managed or converted into useful information. Not only is this expensive and time-consuming, it also works against actually improving quality because the truly important is given the same weight as the trivial. Programs are often implemented in form but not in substance. That is, measuring and reporting take place because this is what the customer is looking for, but the program is not truly integrated with manufacturing and may even be a source of conflict.

Case Example

One of our clients, which supplies the railroad industry, spent thousands of dollars on a mandated quality program that promised to pay for itself by reducing the cost of scrap and rework. When I asked the company's chief executive officer (CEO) how effective the program had been in terms of payback, his response was "pennies." When we investigated why this was so, we found that a quality bureaucracy had been created that was disconnected from the rest of the business. Although the program identified many problems and recommended solutions, that was as far as it went. There was no implementation because the quality effort was not an integral part of managing the company.

There is no quick-fix or magic solution when your company is put at a disadvantage by an extensive quality program that is not working, especially if it is a requirement for doing business with your most important customers. One approach is to separate the truly important quality measures from the trivial, and then concentrate on making these an integral part of your management process. We took this approach with this client and were able to help the company to reduce scrap and rework substantially.

Targeting Rework

Rework is one of the most expensive and damaging forms of waste in any manufacturing operation. It increases costs enormously, consumes otherwise productive capacity, creates extensive delays, and sabotages on-time shipping performance.

Look at it this way, first you pay to make the product incorrectly; then you pay to undo what has been done incorrectly (labor and scrap); then you pay to redo it correctly (more labor and new materials); and during all the time you are undoing and redoing, you are consuming otherwise productive capacity that could have been used to make salable, profitable products (opportunity cost). In effect, you are paying four or more times the standard cost of production for items that have to be reworked. It makes good sense, therefore, to put rework on the top of your list as a target for continuous improvement. (By the way, this problem is not fixed by exhorting people to "do it right the first time.")

Closing the Loop

As strange as it may seem, it is not uncommon to find companies that lack the systems and information required to know whether money was made or lost on an order. Failing to "close the loop" refers to a gap that exists in the management process. If you are not routinely comparing actual costs to the estimate for each order, it is impossible to focus problem solving and continuous improvement on specific areas of need. Were materials costs higher than estimated? Did we have more scrap than expected? Was the actual shop floor routing different from the one used in estimating? Were our labor costs higher than estimated? Why? Without proper information, these questions go unanswered and can happen again and again, order after order, without being corrected.

A primary reason for failing to close the loop is that information systems are fragmented. Sales data may be in one system, estimating in another, production planning in a third, shop floor information may be kept in a manual card file, and accounting data likely resides in yet another system. Without an integrated approach to information management, the task of assembling data for comparison and analysis purposes becomes such an overwhelming task that it doesn't get done.

If you are one of the fortunate few who has a well-integrated computerized information system, you will be able to produce a report that compares estimated to actual costs as soon as an order is on its way to the customer. However, if your shop lacks this capability, you will need another method for capturing and comparing estimated and actual costs for each order.

One solution is to modify your shop router—or traveler, production card, shop ticket, or whatever name your company has for this document. The following example in Figure 5-3 of an actual redesigned router provides some guidance along these lines.

Figure 5-3. Shop router.

L A S E R   SHOP ROUTER

Item Description_____: Circular blade 4.724 diameter; 1.265 six-sided center hole; 25 v-notches rim (same style as item S71138); 3/16 wide double bevel with honed edge.
Finished thickness .050 same as stock received. Materials: 286#, steel code 121513 (.050" x 6 3/8" coil 410 tempered). Requires 46 shipping cartons # 161132 Kraft 5 x 5 x 1.5
Job planner/estimator_____ :J.Doe _____ Customer _____ :xxxxxxxxx _____ Order Value _____ :$$

Order # 623839   Item # S70019   Drawing # S71138   Rev # 01   Qty: 500 +/-5% Start 525   Release: 1/09/98   Promised Ship Date: 1/20/00   Actual Ship Date:_____

Date	Name	Seq.	Opr./Rate	Qty/S	Run Time Plan	Actual	Setup Time Plan	Actual
1/09/98 Setup		9	2598/00		0.00		0.30 W/C 25001	
1/12/98 Cut with laser use program # 4582		10	2500/79		6:58		0:00 W/C 25001	
1/13/98 Glaze remove burr		35	1810/200		2:45		0:00 W/C 193610	
1/13/98 Setup		39	1898/00		0:00		0:05 W/C 189092	
1/14/98 Straighten in rollers .004 F.I.R.		40	1862/325		1:41		0:00 W/C 189092	
1/14/98 Setup		45	1898/00		0:00		0:10 W/C 188621	
1/15/98 Inspect flats, electro etch per drawing location		46	1835/437		1:16		0:00 W/C 188621	
1/15/98 Setup		49	1898/00		0:00		0:20 W/C 183402	
1/19/98 Precision grind bevels 3/16 double bevel .004/006 on edge 12 degrees incl.		50	1822/65		8:28		0:20 W/C 183402	
1/19/98 Setup		69	1898/00		0:00		0:17 W/C 183441	
1/20/98 Hone on Sputnik		70	1810/143		3:51		0:00 W/C 183441	
1/20/98 Demag/count/wrap/box/tape/label		80	1893/1651		0:20		0:00 W/C 189610	

Total Processing Time: _____ Plan 25:13 _____ Actual: _____   Setup time Plan 1:41   Actual: _____
Materials Usage: _____ Pieces start: 525 _____ Shipped: _____   Scrapped _____   Scrap % _____
On-time Performance: _____ Promised Ship Date: _____ Actual: _____   Actual Ship Date: _____

Explanatory Notes

The header provides the following basic order information:

◆ The LASER stamp indicates the order should start in laser cutting as opposed to the press room.

◆ *Release* refers to the date that the order is scheduled to be released to the shop for production.

◆ *Actual* refers to the date the order was actually received in the shop.

◆ *Qty +/-* refers to the order quantity within an industry standard variance. The nature of this manufacturing process includes a normal scrap allowance of 5 to 10 percent to provide for machine adjustments. This order started with 525 pieces with an expected yield of 500+ shipped.

◆ Other items are self-explanatory.

The item description provides the shop with detailed information about the order, materials required, shipping instructions, and other special requirements. Sometimes this section includes a "heads up" to alert operators to problems that have been experienced in the past.

The balance of the router shows the scheduled process of the order through the shop.

◆ *Date* refers to the date the operation is scheduled to be performed.

◆ *Name* (operator's initials after completing the work).

◆ *Seq* (sequence) is the line in which the operation appears in the routing file.

◆ *Opr/Rate* refers to the operation number and the expected productivity rate for that operation in pieces per hour. If the operation is a setup, 00 is used.

◆ *Qty* refers to the quantity actually produced with /S used to show pieces scrapped at that operation (operator enters data after completing the work).

◆ *Run Time* is the time in hours required to process the order quantity at each operation given the productivity rate. The operator enters the Actual time required.

◆ *Setup Plan* and *Actual* times are self-explanatory.

◆ A line is provided under each operation for special instructions or information.

◆ *W/C* refers to the work center scheduled to perform the operation.

A summary at the bottom provides a ready reference for comparing estimated and actual performance on key indices that include estimated versus actual materials usage, labor hours, and setup times; scrap; and on-time shipping performance. Not only does this router format provide a quick and convenient means for collecting and summarizing information from the floor, it also communicates expectations to operators regarding productivity rates and expected times for completing each operation.

Note: Some people would argue that it is better not to provide operators with this information because they might be able to do an operation faster, and will take the maximum time available. I don't agree with this thinking or what it implies about employees. I know you get better results overall when performance expectations are communicated and don't worry being taken advantage of occasionally.

The Computer Is Not the Solution

Many companies mistakenly assume that a state-of-the-art computer system will solve all their problems. The idea is that so-called better systems will enable management to gain greater control over variables such as order backlog, work in process, or production costs. However, a better system may only enable management to locate an order in process with greater precision, rather than actually improving the ability to get that order through the shop and out the door. A better computer system is not a magic bullet, and a systems improvement approach may only have a limited effect in complex environments that have multiple operations and many orders on the floor at the same time. A computer is a tool that can help you organize and use information more effectively. It is not a cure-all for underlying process, organization, or people problems.

This is not to say that upgrading your computer system is a bad thing to do, or not worthwhile in many cases. However, it can be a knee-jerk reaction that misses the need for more fundamental organizational rethinking, especially since new organizing concepts and perspectives can be powerful drivers for lead-time reduction and profit improvement.

Accelerating Cash Flow

The overall business process is not complete until accounts receivable are converted into cash in the bank. Many shops suffer from insufficient cash flow and an overreliance on expensive working-capital loans or factoring. This problem can be rectified by reducing lead time because less working capital is required when the time from order entry to shipping is compressed (that is, the time from "money out" to "money in" is shortened, which lowers the level of working capital required).

Second, because programs that reduce lead time also reduce costs and improve margins, another source of hidden working capital is released. Finally, insofar as sales improve as a result of shorter lead times, these incremental sales have higher margins, sometimes by as much as 50 percent or more because only variable costs increase, not fixed costs. These higher-margin sales further ease cash-flow problems and improve profitability.

Actions You Can Take

Although reducing lead time improves cash flow, it also makes sense to take direct action in this area. Here are some things to consider:

- ◆ *Get money up front* if you can, or arrange for progress payments based on work completed, instead of waiting to invoice customers upon shipment.
- ◆ *Charge for engineering services.* Often, engineering services are considered part of overhead. Some customers require more than others, which amounts to light users subsidizing heavy users of these services.
- ◆ *Coordinate invoicing with shipping.* Some shops invoice once a month. Consider invoicing as a natural extension of the business process. Coordinate invoicing with shipments so the shipment and the invoice arrive simultaneously.
- ◆ *Call customers* to ensure that the order was received and is satisfactory. It is to your advantage to find out immediately if there is a problem that

will delay payment, rather than waiting for the customer to tell you, and lose valuable time.

◆ *Track outstanding invoices closely* and follow up conscientiously to expedite payments. A call to a customer is more effective than a letter or past-due notice when it comes expediting late payments.

◆ *Charge interest on overdue amounts.* Make certain that you communicate your credit policy clearly when you confirm the order.

Listen to Your Customers

In this customer-driven age, every company must know more about its customers and strive to serve them better. Because job shops go head to head with competitors on every order bid, it makes sense to ask your customers what you can do to serve them better. What do they like about doing business with you? What don't they like? What could you have done better on their most recent order? How can you meet their needs better? Ask, "If we could do one thing that would increase our value to you, what would it be? What do you look for when selecting among competing bids? How many bids do they typically send out? These types of questions yield valuable information you can use to enhance your company's competitive position and grow your business.

Probably the best place to locate responsibility for conducting customer surveys is within your sales or marketing department. This has several advantages, the primary one being that it creates another opportunity for your salespeople to talk to customers. The types of questions outlined above are natural selling questions every salesperson uses in the normal course of doing business and seeking repeat orders.

However, if you are not willing to listen and act on customers' feedback, don't even bother asking—your customers will ask why you're asking them, and your salespeople will be put at an embarrassing disadvantage as well. This is another instance of doing more harm than good by involving people and then ignoring them.

Note: Companies that have traditionally competed solely on price and quality may need to reorient their sales force. Traditionally, commissions are paid on the basis of net sales, which can be a problem. When a salesperson exercises some degree of control over the selling price, there is only a minor incentive to get top dollar for an order. Look at it this way: Why should a salesperson push the envelope on price and risk losing an order on account of the minimal impact the higher price has on his or her commission?

However, when you add speed to your competitive arsenal, you should consider a commission structure that pays salespeople on both sales *and* margins. This commission structure is balanced in such a way that even small margin increases result in larger commissions. Paying on both sales and margins changes the incentive for the salesperson to charge more for the value inherent in the company's ability to reduce lead time. How many times have you paid more to get something faster? For example, you have probably paid more money to use FedEx rather than UPS Ground when you wanted or needed an item quickly.

Key Points

◆ One of the most important steps you can take to position your company for profitable growth is to ensure that your business is properly aligned with its markets and customers.

◆ Videotaping changeovers will enable a company to identify and eliminate delays.

◆ Process-step value analysis will enable you to identify and eliminate non-value-adding activities and move work through your shop more quickly.

◆ When your company is put at a disadvantage by an overdetermined quality program, separate the truly important measures from the trivial, and then concentrate on making these an integral part of your management process.

◆ Put rework at the top of your list as a target for improvement.

◆ If you are not routinely comparing actual costs to the estimate for each order and closing the loop, it is impossible to focus problem solving and continuous improvement on specific areas of need.

◆ A well-designed router is a key source of information for performance improvement.

◆ The computer is not the solution.

◆ The overall business process is not complete until accounts receivable are converted into cash in the bank.

◆ Listen to your customers. Act on what you learn.

N O T E S

CHAPTER SIX

CONTINUOUS IMPROVEMENT

Continuous improvement—along with *pull, flow* and the elimination of waste, or *muda*—is a key concept in lean manufacturing. Continuous improvement is based on the fact that perfection is an ideal, so anything and everything can be improved. It is a philosophical stance that makes sense in a today's business world, which is characterized by fast-paced change, new technologies, and more demanding competitive pressures.

Continuous improvement works best when it is established philosophically, culturally, and operationally as an integral part of managing your business—as opposed to a program that is run on a "sometimes" basis. It can be particularly effective when it is designed to put performance feedback in the hands of operators and first-line supervisors, the people who have the most direct and immediate impact on shop-floor productivity and costs.

Continuous improvement also has implications for how a company perceives and manages change. By its very nature, continuous improvement opposes the *status quo*. A company that has truly internalized continuous improvement—both as a management philosophy and as a way of operating—looks for opportunities to make productive changes, as opposed to resisting these opportunities. Taking a proactive stance when it comes to change is extremely important, especially when a company is under increasing pressure from customers and competitors.

This chapter explains how to install a nonbureaucratic continuous improvement process in a custom manufacturing environment. I use the term *nonbureaucratic* because the approach described here is uncomplicated, practical, and above all, effective. It consists of these basics:

◆ Using a performance improvement team to close the loop by comparing estimated to actual results (see Chapter 5)
◆ Installing a weekly management report, which makes it possible to monitor performance across the entire business process virtually in real time
◆ Graphing trends to show performance improvement over time

What Does Continuous Improvement Look Like?

Continuous improvement is a data-driven methodology that involves an ongoing monitoring of performance combined with the never-ending pursuit of improvement. Figure 6-1 shows a performance improvement team using a continuous improvement process.

Using Performance Improvement Teams to Drive Continuous Improvement

Because most business problems and improvement efforts involve more than one area or function in your company, it makes sense to establish a cross-functional performance improvement team(s)—which is sometimes referred to as a process improvement team (PIT)—to focus on specific areas of need. A team can have permanent members as well as members who participate on an ad hoc basis.

If you only set up one PIT, use it to close the loop at the point in the process where manufacturing is complete and the order has been shipped to the customer so that you achieve maximum leverage for improvement. The router described in Chapter 5 is a key source of information for this team. This PIT operates on an ongoing basis to reduce rework, scrap, and late shipments, as well as to increase productivity, solve problems, and improve margins. The team's working process involves a cycle of thinking/planning, doing, measuring results, and learning as illustrated earlier. Performance improvement is measured in clear and direct ways, and is trended over time to show progress. The team uses histograms, fishbone diagrams, the design of experiments, process analysis, and other tools to analyze data and construct problem solutions. Graphing productivity and performance trends lets team members know whether their solutions are effective or need to be revisited.

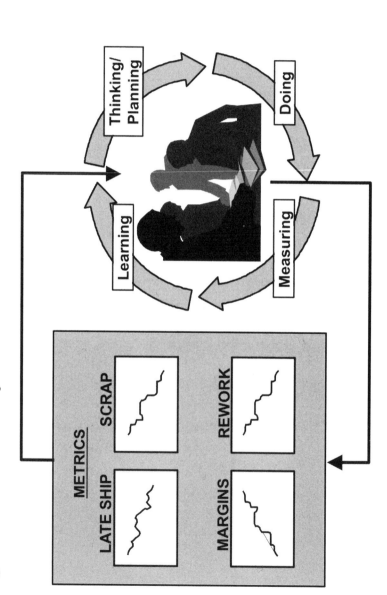

Figure 6-1. What does continuous improvement look like?

To reiterate: If the business system does not provide the means to compare actual costs against the estimate for each order, it is impossible to focus problem solving and continuous improvement on specific areas of need. Were materials costs higher than estimated? Was more scrap produced than expected? Was the actual shop-floor routing different from the one used in estimating? Were labor costs higher than estimated? Why? Without proper information, these questions go unanswered and can happen again and again, order after order, without being corrected.

In order to be effective, this PIT must have a mandate to operate beyond manufacturing to encompass the business process as a whole. For example, what if the team discovers that the routing used in estimating is not the one actually used to manufacture the product on the floor? It would be necessary for the PIT to reconcile this difference, and that would involve working with the estimating department.

It is not unusual for a PIT to find that rework is being caused by inaccurate, out-of-date, illegible, or incomplete information coming from the front office. (When you are already half way through the manufacturing process, it is too late to find out that the latest version of the print did not go out on the floor with the order.) The team must have a mandate to go beyond manufacturing to work with office staff to improve the quality of information being sent to the floor.

In one case, a performance improvement team discovered that proper preventive maintenance was not being performed on a machine, which led to excessive downtime. Team members had to work outside the bounds of manufacturing to find out why the machine was not being properly maintained to correct the situation.

In another case, a PIT was investigating a rework and scrap problem in a heat-treating operation. Team members found the process could not hold the Rockwell, or hardness, standards specified by the customer. This resulted in hand sorting and testing individual blanks, and reprocessing those that fell outside the specified range. The team came up with a novel solution. Team members asked the customer if the range as specified was absolutely critical. It turned out this standard was set more-or-less arbitrarily, and was redefined more broadly. This eliminated the problem because their heat-treat process could now perform within the wider tolerance range. A portion of the savings was returned to the customer in the form of a price reduction on future orders. Again, this example illustrates the importance of not limiting a PIT to manufacturing *per se*.

Establishing a Performance Improvement Team

A cross-functional performance improvement team needs a certain amount of training to perform effectively. A team needs a focus, or mission, to guide its activities. Members must understand how to measure performance and be able to interpret quantitative feedback. They must learn how to use a few problem-solving tools, as well as be able to conduct effective working sessions. The team must have sufficient organizational clout to promote the adoption and implementation of its ideas and recommendations. For example, if rework is targeted for reduction, the team determines where it is happening and what is causing it, and then works with the operators and supervisors in that portion of the process to eliminate or reduce it.

Since PITs are most effective when they have the backing of the president or owner and senior managers, some companies establish executive-level steering teams that provide guidance, actively review results, and facilitate the implementation of specific recommendations. Without higher-level support and active participation on the part of the executive group, changes will not be implemented and results will be minimal.

Taking a half-hearted approach to improvement will further undermine your efforts in the future by disillusioning employees and making them more skeptical. Employees in companies that have experienced a number of "flavor of the month" fad improvement programs develop a defensive reaction—they keep their heads down, try not to get too involved, pay lip service to the party line, and wait for it to go away. They have learned an important lesson: "This too shall pass."

Note: The technique of using a cross-functional team to close the loop at the point in the process where manufacturing is complete and the order has been shipped to the customer should not be confused with the technique of margin analysis. Margin analysis looks at two things:

1. The difference between the estimated cost and the price (the mark up)
2. The difference between the selling price and the actual cost (the real margin)

Margin analysis will tell you if your sales force is giving away the store or if manufacturing is tremendously inefficient, but it does not provide a method or set of tools for actually changing the conditions that are producing the substandard performance.

A Continuous Improvement Caveat

As a manager you have to be careful not to react negatively when opportunities for improvement surface. This is easy to do because every improvement is also a criticism of past methods by comparison. When a manager says something like, "Why wasn't this done sooner?" or "Who is responsible for this stupidity?"—especially when an improvement is obvious—it can have a chilling effect, and people will be unwilling to risk coming forward with more ideas. In effect, the originator gets slammed for finding a better way instead of being rewarded. If a low level of trust exists in your organization and the proper climate for continuous improvement has not been established, it is unlikely that employees will risk getting blamed, looking bad, or being criticized for efforts to improve. Coach Bear Bryant's maxim, "I'd rather be ruined by praise than saved by criticism," is not a bad thing to keep in mind when promoting continuous improvement in your organization.

Installing a Weekly Management Report

The second requirement for establishing a continuous improvement infrastructure in your company is the installation of a weekly management report. As discussed in Chapter 2, cutting lead time to improve performance and profitability is based on looking at your business as a process that converts quotes into cash. When you view and manage your business as a process, you will be in a better position to pinpoint areas for improvement and act on them more precisely. This perspective can be put into practice by installing a weekly management report, which is a powerful tool that will enable you to monitor your business virtually in real time.

Imagine that you are driving in unfamiliar territory and come to a fork in the road. You want to remain on Route 86, but there is no sign at the fork. You take a chance and turn to the right. You drive ten miles down the road looking for a route marker (see Figure 6-2.) All of a sudden you see a sign that says Route 55. Wrong road! Now you have to drive ten miles back and take the other fork. You have driven twenty miles out of your way, plus you have lost the opportunity value of not being twenty miles further toward your destination.

Suppose, however, that you only drove fifty yards down the road before you saw the Route 55 sign. Now you would have only a hundred-yard inconvenience instead of a twenty-mile problem. This is the basic idea behind the weekly management report—it provides the president and members of the management team with important performance information every week. Obviously, the faster you recognize a problem, the faster you can act to solve it. Therefore, the primary purpose of the weekly management report is to provide business-critical information as quickly as possible.

Note: If you are only using your financial statements to evaluate and monitor business performance, you are using information that is six weeks old or more—from the first week in the month plus two weeks in account-

Figure 6-2. Does this look familiar?

ing to prepare the statement before you see it. When something in your business is going south, using six-week-old information to detect the problem is the same as driving ten miles down the wrong road before you see the route marker.

Information typically included in a management report can be in operational terms (the number of sales calls made on new customers this week or the number of orders shipped on time); dollars (the value of bids submitted this week or sales dollars booked); or percentages (the percent of orders shipped on time or the rework as a percent of total labor hours paid). The management report is aligned with the income statement, and foreshadows it. The information provided by the weekly management report is a leading indicator of the monthly income statement that follows. When a series of good management reports indicates a healthy business process, the financials will follow suit.

How to Construct a Weekly Management Report

The word *construct* is used to indicate the importance of building a management report that makes sense for your business. Although management reports for job shops and other made-to-order operations will contain similar indices, the process of thinking through what you want to measure and why you need to measure it is a valuable exercise for any management team.

A management report is constructed to mirror key indicators for every major step in the overall business process. The report enables management to stay on top of changes from week to week, as well as to monitor overall business performance. Figure 6-3 shows the relationship of a weekly management report to the business process.

The first step in constructing a weekly management report is to outline your business process in a manner similar to Figure 6-3. Assemble your key people and talk through what you think would be important to measure at various points in the process and why. The tendency will be to measure too many things; therefore, you must establish a constraint. A good one is to limit the management report to one side of a standard sheet of 8 1/2- by 11-inch paper, not including graphs. To keep all the information on one sheet of paper, you must set priorities and force choices.

Note: There are system levels in every organization. Metrics that do not fit this top-level weekly management report may be important to capture at the next level. For example, a financial manager may be interested in tracking changes in inventory investment, whereas a materials manager would want information about the quantity and types of materials on hand.

Example of a Weekly Management Report

There are a variety of ways to configure a weekly management report. The following example in Table 6-1, which is typical, is based on an Excel® spreadsheet. Comparative data and graphs are updated automatically when data for the current week are entered. In this example, performance for the current week (#4) is compared with an average week. Year-to-date progress is shown in column #5. Column #6 shows the annual run rate, which includes year-end projections at current

(text continues on page 98)

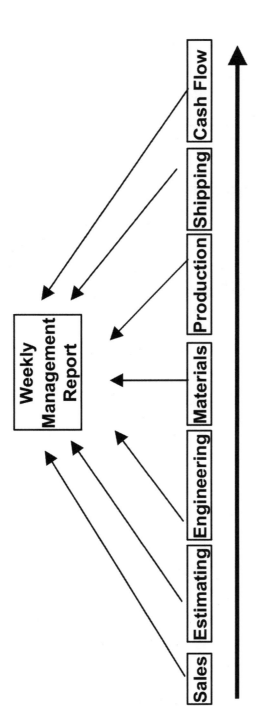

Figure 6-3. Relationship of a weekly management report to the business process.

Table 6-1. Example of a weekly management report.

WEEK # 4		WEEKLY MANAGEMENT REPORT		W/E DATE:	
Percent of Year Elapsed	8%	*Week 4*	*Average*	*YTD*	*Annual*
W/E Date:		(Current)	Week	Cumulative	Run Rate
SALES					
Orders Booked	$	$135,000	$165,000	$660,000	$8,580,000
Orders Shipped (Sales)	$	$180,000	$160,000	$640,000	$8,320,000
Order Backlog	$	$480,000	$502,500	$2,010,000	
ESTIMATING					
RFQs Received	#	48	46	183	2379
Bids Sent On-Time	%	88%	90%		
Orders Won	#	13	13	53	689
Hit Rate	%	27%	29%		
Dollars Won/ Dollars Bid	%	28%	24%		
ENGINEERING					
New Projects	#	5	3	11	143
Completed This Week	#	4	4	15	195
Completed on Schedule	#	4	3	10	130
Backlog Hours	#	20	60	240	3120
Projects Past Due	#	2	3	12	156
RAW MATERIALS INVENTORY					
Materials Received	$	$47,000.00	$43,000	$172,000	$2,236,000
Released to Production	$	$40,000.00	$42,750	$171,000	$2,223,000
Current Inventory	$	$238,000.00	$236,750	$947,000	
Late Vendor Shipments	#	4	3	10	130

PREPRODUCTION					
Orders Released to Shop	#	12	14	57	728
Late Orders to Shop	%	17%	21%		
PRODUCTION					
Labor Efficiency	%	92%	89%		
Rework Hours	#	60	171	685	8905
Rework Cost	$	$600	$775	$3,100	$40,300
Scrap	%	8%	8%		
QUALITY					
Nonconforming Instances	#	3	3	13	169
Customer Complaints	#	3	2	9	117
SHIPPING PERFORMANCE					
Orders Shipped	#	18	14.50	58.00	754
Orders Shipped On-Time	%	88%	85%		
Over Estimate	#	8	6.00	24.00	312
CASH FLOW					
Cash Received	$	$125,000	$143,750	$575,000	$7,475,000
Disbursements	$	$135,000	$141,500	$566,000	$7,358,000
Working Capital	$	$243,000	$242,750	$971,000	

year-to-date performance levels. The report can be easily configured to show progress against a plan or budget, last year's performance, or other comparative bases.

You may choose to add additional columns to show variances (for example, comparisons to the same period last year), progress in achieving annual goals, or comparison to a base. If you are 70 percent through the year (Week #37/52 =71 percent) and only at 50 percent of your sales goal, you may have a problem unless seasonal factors kick in. With a management report in place, you would easily have spotted a sales lag at 20 percent of the year (Week #10) and had the remainder of the year to bring sales back in line with your annual goal. The weekly management report is a flexible tool that is easily tailored to your fit business and management preferences.

The weekly management report can be tied into your company's normal goal-setting process. Many annual goals can be broken down into monthly and weekly increments and should reflect seasonality in your business—that is, a weekly or monthly goal is not necessarily the annual goal divided by fifty-two. Goals should be realistic, attainable, and have a plan for achievement, otherwise they do more harm than good.

Graphs are also updated automatically when data for the current week are entered—a new bar is added each week. This feature enables trends to be monitored, and the results of continuous improvement efforts to be evaluated. (Note that fifty-two data points provide more information at a faster rate than twelve monthly reports.) The three examples in Figure 6-4 show order backlog, rework, and on-time shipment trends.

Selecting the Metrics

The term *metrics* has recently come into popular use. Other terms include *performance indicators, critical success factors, key indices*, and similar variations. The basic idea is to select those measures that most represent important factors in your business. The span should be inclusive—from sales through cash flow—so you can monitor the process as a whole, in addition to monitoring the performance levels of individual process steps. To reiterate, getting your management team together to decide which metrics to include is an extremely valuable exercise for any company.

Installing the Management Report

All you have done up to this point is to determine the metrics and tailor the format to your preferences. The live information that you need will not automatically jump onto the paper. The management report must be installed before it can become an effective tool. The following seven installation steps are required:

1. *Assign responsibility for collecting data and publishing the report to one person.* This individual can be in accounting, the production office, part of the clerical staff, or elsewhere in your organization. The person should be computer literate and know how to use a spreadsheet program.
2. *Determine sources of data and who is responsible for providing these to the publisher.* Make certain that each person in sales, estimating, engineering, etc. understands what data he or she is expected to provide, when, and in what form. Expect some resistance because performance measurement may

Figure 6-4. Graphs generated by the weekly management report.

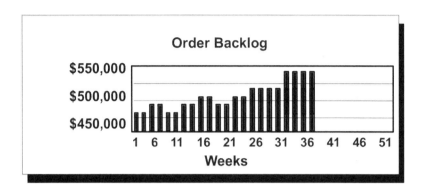

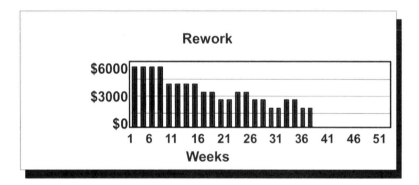

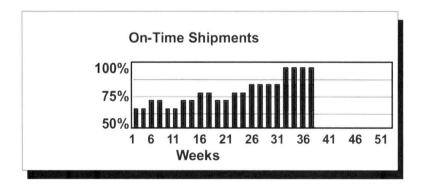

be a new experience for some people in your organization.

3. *Determine when to publish the report.* What day of the week is best for your company to publish and review the management report? One approach is to capture data for the previous week, prepare the report on Monday morning, and conduct a review meeting on Monday afternoon or Tuesday morning. However, this schedule may not fit the normal activity flow for your business. It may be better to capture data from the previous Friday through Thursday of the current week, prepare the report on Friday morning, and conduct your review meeting in the afternoon.

4. *Set the wheels in motion.* Have a kick-off meeting with the publisher and those who are responsible for providing data. Make certain that everyone understands the need to provide accurate information on time so that the report is ready for the senior management review meeting. The publisher will need top management's support to get the job done, and a kick-off meeting is an excellent way to demonstrate management's commitment.

5. *Build as you go.* Recognize that you will not publish a complete report the first time out. Some data will be difficult to access and will be missing initially. Do not wait until you have a report that is 100 percent perfect before you start using it. It should take no more than a week to do everything necessary to produce the first report. You may already have a similar report in place. Take this opportunity to upgrade it, and make certain that it is used as an integral part of your management system.

6. *Refine and upgrade.* As you start to use the report, the original metrics you decided to include may

not be as useful in practice as they first appeared. Do not be afraid to modify, add, or remove metrics as you go along. Also, some metrics may only be useful for a limited period of time (for example, to monitor a particular business condition or short-term problem). The weekly management report is a flexible tool that can be easily tailored to fit your business and preferences.

7. *Use the report.*

How to Use the Management Report

The purpose of the management report is to provide the management team with immediate information that indicates the status of your business. It enables you to pinpoint problems and areas for improvement sooner rather than later. However, the report itself only provides information. It is up to the management team to interpret this information and act on it. Figure 6-5 illustrates how the weekly management report can be integrated into your business process to drive continuous improvement.

Note: The management report can be an excellent communications tool for informing employees about how the company is doing, which areas are in need of improvement, and the progress that is being made. How widely you choose to disseminate this information will depend on how open you are with sharing information in your company.

The weekly performance review meeting should follow a standard agenda:

1. Review the weekly numbers and trends (graphs).
2. Interpret and determine actions to be taken.

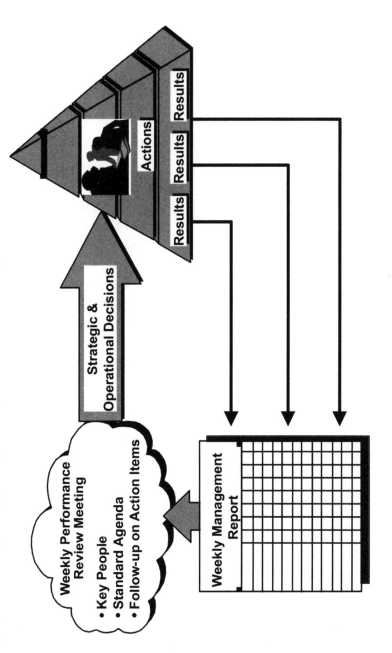

Figure 6-5. Using a weekly management report to drive continuous improvement.

3. Action update (for example, each member of the team reports on progress made or problems encountered in completing previous assignments).
4. Assign new responsibilities as required with expected completion times.
5. Document and publish these assignments—maintain a log of action items so assignments don't fall through the cracks.

Key Points

◆ Continuous improvement is based on the fact that perfection is an ideal; therefore, anything and everything can be improved. It works best when established philosophically and operationally as an integral part of managing your business.

◆ Companies that adopt a continuous improvement philosophy and approach seek out opportunities for improvement, rather than resist change.

◆ A nonbureaucratic continuous improvement framework includes a performance improvement team to close the loop in combination with a one-page weekly management report. Graphs show performance trends.

◆ The management report foreshadows the monthly financials. It is based on the concept of accelerating performance reporting, which includes operational as well as financial information.

◆ Although management reports for job shops and other made-to-order operations contain similar indices, the process of thinking through what you want to measure and why is a valuable exercise for any management team.

◆ Limiting the report to a single page is an effective way to counter the tendency to measure everything. Metrics that do not fit this report can be captured at the next organizational level.

◆ The management report must be installed and used. Follow the steps outlined previously to implement this valuable tool.

NOTES

CHAPTER SEVEN

IMPLEMENTATION

Chapter 6 described how to implement a weekly management report and close the loop by using a performance improvement team. These are essential first steps in improving the performance of your business and positioning it for profitable growth. Be advised, however, the industrial landscape is littered with failed programs that promised big results and produced very little because they were not implemented or "fell out." The inability to implement is most often the weakest link in any company's efforts to make changes that would improve business performance. This chapter addresses the difficulties of implementation in more detail, such as why implementations fail and what you can do to be more successful.

Implementation Defined

To say that a change has been implemented or installed—the terms are often used interchangeably—in your organization means it has become a routine, functioning part of your business that adds value. For example, you could reasonably say the weekly management report is installed when it is published on time every week, is accurate and up-to-date, distributed to everyone who is supposed to get it, reviewed in a management meeting, and acted upon appropriately to drive corrective actions and continuous improvement. In other words, the production, distribution, and use of the management report has become a reliable routine in your organization that is sustained because people recognize its value and it is used to run the business.

Conversely, if you need to oversee that the report actually gets produced and distributed then, according to this definition, it is not implemented or installed. It is also important to recognize the need to "install" the concept and value of a management report—or any change—not merely the mechanics. If managers and other employees in your company do not recognize the value and/or do not act on this information to correct problems and drive continuous improvement, the report will probably fall out because it is not perceived as having any value or functional utility.

The whole business comes together in this report since it reflects the entire process from sales to cash. The trick is to understand the *meaning* of the numbers, not merely the numbers themselves. We implemented a weekly management report for a manufacturing client in 1985. Key people review it religiously every week in a meeting and could not imagine running their business without it.

Requirements for Effective Implementation

Implementation is a detail-oriented and time-consuming effort. You will be more effective when you ensure these basic requirements are met.

Start Small

Once you have the weekly management report installed and published for the first time, which also means you have determined the key indices for your business and how to measure them, the next step is to start the process of taking delays out of your business process. A good place to start is at the point where requests for quotations are received through estimating up to the point where the order is won or lost.

The logic for starting here is threefold:

1. A company that can get its quote in front of a customer before anyone else has a higher probability of winning that order.
2. This part of the process is straightforward. (Use the process analysis tools described in Part III.)
3. This process has probably been ignored in your company; therefore, it is fertile ground for improvement.

Note: You may have already implemented some form of process analysis or process improvement in your company, likely in conjunction with a quality program. Chances are you did not recognize the need to eliminate chronological delays in these processes—that is, the focus was on tasks, documentation, and ensuring compliance. However, you may find that the work you did previously, such as flow charts or live system flows, can be recycled.

Organize for Implementation

You must be organized for implementation in addition to the way you are normally organized to run your business. Typically, teams are formed and assigned to specific areas. Each team should have a designated team leader. In larger companies, a steering team is often formed, which is composed of people who head up the major areas of the business. This helps to ensure that changes in one area are not having unintended effects in other areas. The steering team can also function as the reporting body for implementation teams.

Provide Leadership

The steering team is not a substitute for the leadership provided by the owner or general manager. If the boss is not behind the program and cutting lead time is not a top organizational priority, the chances of accomplishing significant results are slim to none. When the boss doesn't think a program is truly important, the organization's members sense this indifference. They may pay lip service to the program, but they usually keep their heads down and wait for it to go away. This is why consultants and other change agents insist on top management's visible involvement and commitment because they know the program will fail without it. On the other hand, change can fail when it is imposed from the top, especially when the effort lacks meaningful involvement of key people throughout the organization. This can be a difficult balance to strike.

Ensure Understanding and Commitment among Key People

If your management team is fragmented and not thinking in systems terms—that is, everything is connected— you run the risk of isolating a program in a functional area and missing the connections to the balance of your organization. For example, suppose you are introducing new equipment on the shop floor that will increase throughput. You also have to crank up the sales effort to ensure the new capacity is sold, ensure you have adequate sources of supply for the additional raw materials you will need, have sufficient storage and materials-handling capability, can train operators to run the new equipment, and perhaps even increase your line of credit with the bank to cover additional working capital requirements. There are few programs isolated in a single department; most have an impact on the organization as a whole.

Develop a Plan and Schedule

Each team should develop a project schedule with tasks, key events, time frames, and individual assignments in those areas designated for improvement. The steering team should construct and monitor an overall project schedule that provides integration for the improvement teams. By ensuring the tasks on this overall schedule are completed and milestones are met, an organization generates the momentum required to move forward in the face of the formidable opposition presented by the *status quo*. On the other hand, the *status quo* also makes the business work, so the idea is not to bash tradition but to think through new ways of doing business. Listen carefully to opposing voices to ensure that all bases are covered.

Maintain Momentum

It is easy to mistake the urgent for the important. The short-term, day-to-day demands of running a business have a tendency to overshadow longer-term improvement initiatives. To paraphrase Gresham's law, "short-term drives out long-term." Once momentum is lost, it is difficult to regain and much valuable time will be lost.

Get Some Help

Many smaller companies, especially job shops, employ fewer than fifty people and have annual revenues that are less than $10 million. Smaller businesses do not have extra resources to devote to organization improvement projects, so the task of implementation falls to managers and other key people. Implementation is a detail-oriented and time-consuming effort, so it is unrealistic to expect quick results because key people already have full-time jobs running the business.

Do-it-yourself programs usually take more time and cost more money than was planned for, especially in terms of the opportunity costs associated with delays in implementing improvements that have a bottom-line payoff. For example, delaying progress on a project with a \$600,000 annual improvement potential costs you a minimum of \$50,000 per month. A little implementation support goes a long way, so don't be penny wise and pound foolish.

Measure Results and Provide Feedback

It is important to measure improvement on key business indicators over time, which is a feature of the graphing capability of the weekly management report. A potential pitfall is that you will spend too much time and effort finding out where you are—by setting baselines and benchmarking your performance—as opposed to focusing your time and energies on getting better. Benchmarking sounds logical but is inconsequential— you are either continuing to improve, or you are not. If you can see a positive trend in key business indicators being sustained over time, what difference does knowing the precise starting point really make?

Providing feedback to those members of the organization who are making these improvements happen (or not) shows you are serious, makes the effort meaningful, and educates people so they can make mid-course corrections as required. Publish the results widely throughout the organization. The weekly management report makes this easy to do.

Avoiding Typical Implementation Pitfalls

Pitfalls can be avoided by knowing what they are beforehand, and not getting blindsided during the implementation process. Here are some common reasons why implementations fail:

◆ *Lack of Skill.* Implementation failures are often blamed on resistance to change on the part of organization members who want to continue business as usual and, therefore, sabotage the change effort. This may be true in some cases, particularly when an individual's job is threatened, but a far more frequent cause of failure can be traced to the fact that organizations just don't know how to implement very well. It is not so much individual resistance that gets in the way but rather it's the routines, values, ideas, and behavior patterns that are at the heart of any organization that are difficult to change—that is, the *status quo.*

Managing organizational improvement programs and ensuring that changes in policies, procedures, methods, concepts, and job duties are put into place operationally is difficult to achieve. Implementation is time consuming, often tedious and detail-oriented, and requires a great deal of communication, coordination, and involvement throughout the organization. Implementation is a skill set in its own right, and should be managed as a project. The idea that you can "implement by memo" is naïve and generally no more effective than wishful thinking.

◆ *Solution in Search of a Problem.* Managers often become caught up in the latest fads and believe that so-called magic bullet solutions will improve business performance and competitiveness. However, if the solution doesn't fit the business, either it will not work or it will not last. Sometimes this is called "the rule of the tool" or "I've got a hammer, and everything looks like a nail."

◆ *Overkill.* It stands to reason that the more complicated a program is, the more difficult it will be to design, implement, and sustain. Many programs are overdesigned and require far more time and effort to implement and maintain than they are worth. Quality programs and certifications are good examples. Most require extensive documentation of policies, procedures, work instructions, deviations from standard, and a host of other reports that are so excessive they amount to overkill and institutionalize the past. Often, these programs are mandated by large customers, therefore, if a supplier does not comply, it will essentially be out of business (for example, ISO). Programs like these are often implemented in form but not in substance. That is, measuring and reporting takes place because this is what the customer looks for; however, the program is not truly integrated with manufacturing operations and may even be an obstacle to achieving company goals.

◆ *Poor Prior Experience.* "Here we go again" is a common sentiment in organizations that have gone through a variety of flavor-of-the-month programs, which lasted for a while and then faded away. When a new program is initiated, everyone expects a repeat of the past, doesn't take it seriously, and, of course, implementation fails. You must address this skepticism and demonstrate your commitment during implementation planning, otherwise, don't bother and save everybody a lot of wasted time and effort.

◆ *Time Frame Too Short.* Typically, new ventures take twice as long and cost twice as much as expected. You can get a better sense of how long a program will take to implement if you have a detailed project schedule that lays out every step, and you tackle the implementation in phases. A good approach is to think in terms of high and low intensity periods. The high-intensity portion of the program is used to get the basics in place; low intensity or follow-on is for adjusting, refining, and problem solving. Again, it is better to start small. Don't bite off more than you can chew.

The manufacturing environment has undergone a major paradigm change during the past thirty years and continues to evolve. We have seen a transformation from rich to lean, push to pull, just-in-case to just-in-time, in-house to outsourced, and top-down command and control to self-managing, horizontal process teams. Suppliers operating in this environment must improve continuously and adapt more efficiently to remain competitive and survive. This means companies can no longer accept implementation as the weak link in improving performance, and must take steps to learn how to implement more quickly and effectively.

Table 7-1 highlights major changes that have occurred in the manufacturing environment.

Key Points

Implementation is a detail-oriented and time-consuming effort. You will be more effective when you recognize that:

◆ To perform better than you are doing now requires purposeful action and organizational change. Business as usual produces results as usual.
◆ The pressure to continuously improve will not go away, and will likely intensify.
◆ You must have a strategy and plan for moving forward.
◆ If you can't measure it, you can't manage it.

Table 7-1. Transition matrix.

Past	Present
Inventory is good.	Inventory is bad.
Customer is peripheral.	Customer is central.
Resource rich.	Resource lean.
Push.	Pull.
Just-in-case.	Just-in-time.
Slower pace.	Faster pace.
Command and control management.	Self-managing teams.
Functional isolation.	Functional integration.
Make in house.	Outsource.
Supplier as adversary.	Supplier as partner.
Capital based.	Knowledge based—intellectual capital.
Compete on price.	Compete on value—price, quality, speed.
Lead time.	Customer wait time.

◆ The *status quo* presents formidable opposition to change and improvement.

◆ You cannot accept implementation as the weak link, but must learn how to manage change more successfully.

And when you utilize:

◆ A sound strategy for achieving results; in this case, the book *Speed to Market.*

◆ Properly organized and trained implementation teams.

◆ A line-item project schedule of tasks and key events.

◆ Ongoing project management and leadership.

◆ A method for measuring results and trending improvements.

◆ Implementation support.

◆ Sufficient time and commitment.

N O T E S

PART II

SOLUTION STRATEGIES FOR COMMON JOB SHOP PROBLEMS

CHAPTER EIGHT

WHEN SCHEDULING IS OUT OF CONTROL

When scheduling is out of control, the production schedule is in a constant state of flux and chaos reigns on the shop floor. This is not an uncommon situation in the job shop world. But this description of the problem is incorrect because it is not scheduling that is out of control, but rather the organization that is out of control. What you see in scheduling is merely a symptom or reflection of a more fundamental set of organizational problems. If you are trying to solve a scheduling problem in your company, you will not be successful because that is not the problem. This chapter offers a perspective on the dynamics of out-of-control scheduling and suggestions for ameliorating it.

Case Example

A real-life example is provided by Beta Machine Company, a screw machine shop, whose most pressing need was to get its scheduling under control. By using an Ishakawa fishbone problem-solving method, the company identified more than sixty separate conditions that disrupted its schedule—from late delivery of materials to employee absenteeism—and then set about trying to resolve them. After a year of concentrated work, guess what? Scheduling was still out of control.

Note: It is important to recognize that there are many degrees of being out of control. Some change is to be expected in a job shop. It comes with the territory. But when the frequency or magnitude of disruption exceeds a certain tolerance or comfort level in a particular company, then scheduling is deemed to be *out of control*, as defined by that organization. In other words, there is not some absolute number of schedule changes that define an out-of-control condition.

Schedule Defined

Webster defines the word *schedule* as a list of times of recurring events (for example, a train schedule) or "projected operations." Projected means in the future, so a schedule is a plan for the timing of operations or activities to take place in the future. In effect, a job shop schedule is a forward look. The purpose of the schedule is to show the best way to convert the order backlog through the various shop operations as efficiently as possible, while at the same time meeting customer requirements and promised ship dates.

Static Scheduling

The typical scheduling paradigm used in manufacturing is to view the schedule as a rigid timetable to which the shop is expected to adhere. The schedule is "the boss" and has authority over the floor. This concept of scheduling has its roots in the world of mass production where change is less intense. But this static or one-way concept of scheduling is borrowed from a different type of manufacturing, and is not in accord with the reality of a constantly changing, dynamic, job shop environment. It is the wrong paradigm.

The Fallacy of Static Scheduling

A typical job shop schedule could contain an entry to start Job #00-450 on machine #7 on Monday morning at 8:00 a.m. with an expected run time of six hours. This is the plan. However, there is some probability that Job #00-450 will not run on machine #7 at 8:00 a.m. because there are several contingent events that must also take place for that to happen:

◆ The previous job must have been completed and off the machine.
◆ The material must be available at the machine— contingent upon vendor reliability, completion of upstream operations, and materials management.

◆ The tooling must be available and capable, and the machine set up properly.

◆ The machine itself must be operational.

◆ The operator must be present and capable of performing the work.

◆ The most current information on how to do the job must be available (for example, traveler, specs, prints).

◆ The capacity on the machine or work center must be available and not have been commandeered by a hotter job.

Each of these requirements is also dependent upon its own set of contingencies, for example, the chain of events that must occur for the material to be at the machine at the scheduled time or for the tooling to be available and capable. The greater the number of requirements or contingent events that must take place in order for the job to run on time, and the larger and more complex the systems involved—the greater the probability of system failures, which appear as schedule "misses."

Furthermore, the schedule entry to start job #00-450 on Monday at 8:00 a.m. is only one of many other operations scheduled to take place during the period covered by the schedule. And although there is some probability that any specific operation will not take place as planned, there is an absolute certainty that some scheduled operations will fail to occur on time. In other words, it is a safe bet that your production schedule will be disrupted and require modification, sometimes several times during the same day.

This is neither the fault of the people nor the scheduling system. It is simply the result of probability operating in complex systems, which makes them unreliable. Any schedule, no matter how accurate it may be initially, quickly becomes obsolete when contingent systems fail.

Note: Some of these contingent systems are so reliable they are invisible. For example, electricity must be available to power the machine. This is a highly reliable system that causes few if any schedule misses.

When scheduled operations cannot take place, adjustments are made on the floor in real time—for example, reassigning the operator or running another job on that machine. When this happens, the schedule is no longer accurate. When too many changes of this type occur, the schedule may even lose its ability to function as a plan. The tendency to regard your schedule as a static or one-way plan, which the shop must follow religiously, is not realistic and can be the source of many problems.

The Concept of Dynamic Scheduling

There is an old saying salespeople are fond of using: "Plan your work, work your plan." The belief is that scheduled appointments will be cancelled or changed because this happens frequently. It is up to the salesperson to "work the plan." That is, he or she must make necessary adjustments to be as productive as possible, which is essential for salespeople who are paid on a commission basis. The same idea of "plan your work, work your plan" is the essence of dynamic scheduling in a job shop environment.

Dynamic scheduling recognizes that a relationship exists between the schedule and the reality of changing conditions on the shop floor. Where static or one-way scheduling seeks to dictate what should happen on the floor and when, dynamic scheduling accepts the fact that changes are inevitable and must be accommodated. In dynamic scheduling, planning or developing the schedule is no less rigorous, but changes are expected and integrated into an ongoing, dynamic cycle. Or, as Publilius Syrus, a philosopher in the first century B.C., said, "It is a bad plan that admits of no modification."[1]

Change Your Paradigm

Thus, one of the first issues that must be addressed to get scheduling under control is to change your scheduling paradigm from static to dynamic. This may be easier said than done because the static paradigm is familiar and offers the illusion of control. And because managers, like everyone else, want to feel as if they are in control of events, it may be difficult to give up the old paradigm because it provides a level of comfort. Sometimes the illusion of control is as good as it gets.

Fix Organization Disconnects

Not infrequently, an organization disconnect exists between the scheduler and the production superintendent. This can be apparent in many forms: poor communications, conflicts, or even disregard for the scheduler. This disconnect may be perceived in the organization as a personality conflict, but it is more likely the result of organizational misalignments and a lack of role clarity.

Obviously, a poor relationship between the scheduler and the superintendent on the floor severely undermines the scheduling process. It is not uncommon, for example, to find that changes made on the floor are not regularly communicated to the scheduler. These changes may result from perfectly legitimate reasons, but if the scheduler is not aware that changes have been made, he or she is working under a false set of assumptions regarding available capacity and job progress. Therefore, any new schedule based on these false assumptions will be virtually worthless as a plan since it does not reflect reality.

The effects of this disconnect are compounded when the shop superintendent sees the schedule or scheduler as exerting excessive influence over his or her authority to run the shop. And because the floor is dynamic with many changes, it is easy to disregard the schedule because it is inaccurate the minute it is published. When scheduling is disconnected from the reality of the floor, the schedule no longer functions as a plan for the future, but merely acts as a recording device for the changes that have already been made on the floor. In these cases, the schedule brings up the rear as opposed to showing the way.

When a disconnected relationship exists, it is imperative to fix it so that the scheduler and shop superintendent can work together toward their common objective: To convert the order backlog through the various shop operations as efficiently as possible, while at the same time meeting customer requirements and promised ship dates.

Scheduling Is Not a Clerical Activity

Another difficulty arises when scheduling is perceived as a clerical activity, which it is not, and the scheduler is located in an office area far from the floor, which is often an indicator of an organizational disconnect. If the scheduler does not understand how the shop works, or does not know which machines are best for certain types of work, or does not understand which operators are capable of performing specific operations, and lacks knowledge of other production details, then the schedule is more likely to be disregarded because it lacks common sense.

Develop a Scheduling Strategy

Another issue that must be addressed is to decide on scheduling strategy. What is going to be scheduled and to what level of detail? There are many factors involved in thinking this through, including the complexity of the manufacturing process, the nature of market demand and customer expectations, competitive factors, the frequency of changes initiated by customers, and other variables. In general, the schedule should be constructed to provide the broadest strategic perspective, while the shop floor operates on a tactical level, in an Eisenhower-Patton type relationship. If these domains are not clearly defined and bounded, conflict can easily result.

Managing Extensive and Complex Manufacturing Processes

Although there are wide variations in manufacturing technologies, equipment, and capabilities among companies, a typical metal-working process can include forming (stamping, laser cutting, casting, or machining); tempering (heat treating and curing); secondary operations (grinding, polishing, plating, truing, and testing); and components assembly. Some shops will encompass this entire range, while others may specialize in particular areas and outsource others, such as heat treating or powder coating. Generally speaking, the more extensive and complex the process, the more difficult it is to organize and manage effectively. In complex situations, it is important to think in terms of a scheduling strategy first. The mechanics of scheduling are secondary.

Case Example

A company that serves the aerospace and other high-tech industries has an extensive manufacturing process that begins with pattern-making (using a lost wax process), mold-making, and a foundry that feeds downstream machining, finishing, testing, and assembly operations. In addition, the high-tech nature of the work requires extensive in-process quality control procedures and nondestructive testing. Rework is common. Because orders tended to be in process for extended periods of time, even months in some cases, customers would continually change priorities. As a result, the shop was constantly rescheduling, reprioritizing, and expediting orders. This created much confusion, start-and-stop production, increased costs, undermined quality, and extended delivery schedules.

This company was able to realize significant lead-time reductions, improve customer service, and reduce costs by separating its overall process into two parts, rather than trying to manage an order all the way through in a linear fashion.

Patterns, model-making, and casting (the front end) were scheduled based on customers' requested delivery dates. Once these operations had been completed, the order was then rescheduled through the balance of the process. (The company described its strategy as "pushing it in the front and pulling it out the back.") This enabled the company to reprioritize schedules in response to changes in customer's requirements after castings were complete, but before they entered the next stage of operations. Although this required an interim work-in-process (WIP) build or staging, the overall WIP was reduced because orders flowed through the shop more quickly, and customers had a smaller window of opportunity to change priorities and delivery dates.

Note: Many shop owners believe that buying a new and improved computer system will solve scheduling problems. When this doesn't happen as expected, the tendency is to blame the system or the people or the customers. How many times have you heard, or even said, "If people would just follow the schedule, everything would be fine." Unfortunately, it is not quite that simple as we have seen.

However, when scheduling strategy and organizational disconnects are addressed, the new computerized shop-management system can be used more effectively. One of the great advantages of a sophisticated shop management system is the ability to regenerate a production schedule with a mouse click. This capability, in concert with effective data collection methods and feedback from the floor, enables the scheduler to run what-if scenarios with more accurate information. In effect, the scheduler is operating closer to reality.

Reducing uncertainty in contingent systems is another advantage of having an integrated computer system in a shop. Because the system is designed to make production requirements more visible, they can be acted upon sooner. For example, when an order is booked and entered into the system, a bill of materials is produced and purchase orders can be generated automatically. The sooner a purchase order is in the hands of a vendor, the greater the probability the materials will be delivered when needed.

Key Points

Static scheduling in a dynamic job shop environment is the wrong paradigm. Scheduling problems will improve, however, when you:

◆ Recognize the uncertain nature of the job shop environment; expect and accept changes.

◆ Adopt the concept of dynamic scheduling, and recognize that the relationship between the schedule and the floor is a dynamic, ongoing loop. Plan your work, work your plan.

◆ Recognize an out-of-control scheduling situation is a symptom of organizational problems.

◆ Fix organizational disconnects. Ensure the scheduler and production superintendent are working in concert, and are not at odds with each other. When scheduling is disconnected from the reality of the floor, the schedule no longer functions as a plan for the future, but merely acts as a recording device for the changes that have already been made on the floor.

◆ Determine a scheduling strategy that fits your organization and business situation. The schedule provides the broader strategic perspective, while the shop floor operates on a tactical level. Develop a scheduling strategy before mechanics.

Reference

1. Rhoda Thomas Tripp, *The International Thesaurus of Quotations* (New York: Thomas Y. Crowell Company, 1970), p. 475. Originally from *Moral Sayings, 1st Century BC*, translated by Darius Lynan.

N O T E S

N O T E S

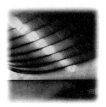

CHAPTER NINE

HOCKEY STICK BLUES

Hockey stick is a term used to describe a pattern common to job shops in which a great effort is expended during the last week of the month to ship as much as possible to "make the numbers." The hockey stick image represents the pattern of more or less equal shipments during the first three weeks of the month with a big spike at the end.

Once established, this pattern is inefficient, costly, and difficult to break. It is very expensive to juggle production orders in the queue, but you will never see these additional costs—and profit erosion—on your income statement because the costs of rescheduling, disruptions, and resulting inefficiencies get lost in the general overhead and labor productivity numbers.

This chapter examines the hockey stick pattern in more depth to gain some insight into its dynamics, and shows how it can be addressed. You may not be able to eliminate it completely, but you can make it less severe, less disruptive, and less costly.

Problem Solving vs. Problem Amelioration

We often think problem solving means problem elimination. A solved problem is one that no longer exists. However, there are certain types of dynamic organizational problems, such as the hockey stick, that cannot be completely eliminated. They can only be ameliorated, that is, made less severe or less frequent. It is important to understand that your assumptions about the nature of a problem will determine your approach to its solution. If you tackle a particular organizational problem and understand it cannot be eliminated but only ameliorated, your approach and expectations will reflect this understanding. You will be far more successful in dealing with it when you understand the reality as opposed to erroneously believing you can solve it by elimination.

Hockey Stick Dynamics

At some point toward the end of the month, management recognizes that sales are running behind and an additional amount must be shipped to make the monthly numbers. A full-court press is mounted to complete orders, pack, ship, and invoice so they can be counted as sales for the current month. The shop knows the drill having done it countless times before. A search for orders on the floor nearest to completion is undertaken. Hot lists are created, production workers are reassigned to handle the additional workload in final production and shipping, overtime is authorized, and a higher level of activity and energy is evident on the floor.

Sometimes customer ship dates are sacrificed as orders closer to completion are moved up in the queue. When a company puts itself ahead of its customers by expediting orders that are closer to completion merely to meet its own internal need to make the numbers, the results can be damaging for the business. The hockey stick syndrome can result in undermining long-term business relationships and growth. As customers become dissatisfied with the company's lack of reliability and on-time ship performance, they simply take their business elsewhere . . . just as you would.

Setting the Stage for the Next Month

Once the "crisis" is passed and a new month starts, employees have a tendency to slack off to compensate for the extra effort expended during the previous week and the pace slows. At the same time, the orders nearest to completion have been sucked out of the production process so there is little to ship in the first week of the new month. You're already behind.

Another complication arises when production workers, who are normally assigned to the front end of the process—for example, shear and brake in a sheetmetal operation—are reassigned to handle the extra workload in final production and shipping. This means a lower volume of new work was started during the last week of the month. A vacuum or "hole" is created in the flow of work through the shop. Unbalancing the workflow in this manner creates its own set of inefficiencies and contributes to setting the stage for a repetition of the hockey stick next month.

There may also be a psychological payoff from the hockey stick that arises from the challenge it represents. People often feel good and gain a sense of accomplishment when they achieve a difficult goal. The last week of the month challenge the hockey stick represents may serve this purpose in some shops.

A Combination of Factors

The hockey stick pattern results from a combination of self-reinforcing, dynamic factors that make it difficult to break. These include:

◆ Sucking work out of the final stages of the production process, thus creating a shipping vacuum for the next week or two

◆ Failing to start a sufficient volume of work as a result of reassigning front-end and other production people to final operations, thus creating a lower volume of input

◆ The natural tendency for people to take a break after a period of heightened activity and extra effort

◆ Accepting the hockey stick as normal because it is familiar

◆ The power of the pattern to replicate itself since the previous month sets the stage for the next month

◆ The lack of a clear solution hampered by the belief that problem solving means problem elimination

◆ The psychological payoff

What You Can Do

There is no question that the hockey stick, once established as an organizational dynamic, is difficult to resolve. Part of the problem lays in the monthly accounting model common to virtually every business and the importance of making the monthly numbers.

Following this logic, therefore, the weekly numbers are as important to the monthly numbers as the months are to the year, so the first step in dealing with the hockey stick is to change your perspective from months to weeks. Make the weekly ship goals, and the month will follow suit.

This is obvious, but not easy. One difficulty is that most companies do not have an organized approach for measuring key performance indicators on a weekly basis. The typical method is for the person who wants the information to collect a hodge-podge of data from various sources, then try to assemble these data into a coherent picture of the business.

Install a Weekly Management Report

Thus, the first step in ameliorating the hockey stick is to implement a weekly management report, which is described in Chapter 7. Recall that this report provides performance-related operational information across the entire business process. And because it is published weekly, it acts as an early warning system to detect problems so they can be addressed before becoming more severe. The weekly management report can be constructed to show weekly shipments and volumes entered into production, one key to minimizing this problem.

Adopt a Weekly Focus

A shop that has annual revenues of $8 million ships approximately $670,000 per month, or $168,000 per week, on average. Table 9-1 illustrates what happens when a shop falls behind its weekly shipping goals. In this example, approximately half of the total for the month must be shipped in the last week to make the goal—$168,000 for the fourth week plus the $164,000 not shipped previously.

Table 9-1. When a shop falls behind its weekly shipping goals.

	Week 1	Week 2	Week 3	Week 4	Month Total
Plan Ship	$168,000	$168,000	$168,000	$168,000	$670,000
Actual Ship	$ 70,000	$120,000	$150,000	$332,000	$?
Remainder	$ 98,000	$146,000	$164,000	$?	

Contrast this scenario with a shop operating on a weekly time frame, as shown in Table 9-2, where missed shipping dollars from the previous week are brought forward. If the goal for week one is not achieved, then the focus shifts to week two and the goal is updated. This method establishes a new, more accurate weekly goal, and provides heightened visibility at week two. This is better than ignoring the situation until week four and then going into crisis mode. Even if you don't catch up in weeks two and three, focusing on weekly increments dramatically increases the probability that you will be further ahead toward your monthly goal.

Table 9-2. When a shop operates on a weekly time frame.

	Week 1	Week 2	Month Total
Plan Ship	$168,000	$266,000	$670,000
Actual Ship	$ 70,000		
Remainder	$ 98,000		

Input Control

A second contributor to the hockey stick is the failure to start a sufficient volume of work at the beginning of the production process because front-end people have been reassigned to final operations and shipping. This situation can also be ameliorated by using a weekly management report. It is a simple matter to measure and monitor the volume of work entered into production each week. If you are not starting with the correct volume, you will not have the work in process to complete and ship. The phrase "entered into production" means through the first operation because merely releasing orders to the floor means nothing if they are not acted upon.

In addition, if you have pulled all the work out of the back end of the shop to make the previous month's numbers, how do you make the first week's goals? There is nothing there to complete and ship. And if you have reassigned front-end people to final operations and shipping, which stalls the start of new orders, you have severely unbalanced the workflow through the shop and set the stage for replicating the hockey stick.

Use Information Appropriately

Changing your perspective from monthly to weekly and having an organized method for producing a weekly management report will not, in and of itself, have any impact on the hockey stick. You have to understand the implications of the information the report provides and then act accordingly. For example, it may still be necessary to reassign front-end people to handle the extra workload in final operations and shipping, only now you are more aware of the time and impact.

So rather than general assignments such as, "Hey Mike, how about going down to shipping and helping them get the orders out." You might say, "Hey Mike, can you help out in shipping for a couple of hours and then do the shearing on that Amalgamated order so we can get it into production?" The point is that when you understand the dynamics of the hockey stick, you can see the effects of rescheduling and reassigning people more clearly, and, therefore, you can address production needs more precisely.

Incremental Work-Out Strategy

The hockey stick is not the type of problem that can be solved once and for all with a dramatic solution. If you think the problem will be solved by taking a hit in one month—for example, not going into crisis mode and continuing production as usual—you will find that this solution only provides temporary relief. Before you know it, the pattern will reassert itself because you have not addressed the underlying need to manage the process and focus on weekly increments.

The solution strategy for ameliorating the hockey stick is incremental. By being aware of the weekly goals and shipping a little more each week to catch up, less is required to be shipped during the last week of the month. This, in turn, reduces the magnitude of the crisis and its corresponding level of disruption.

Also, when you pull less work out of the finishing stages of the production process in week four, you will be able to ship more in the first part of the following month. When you are aware of how much work is actually being entered into production each week, as well as shipped, this will help ensure a sufficient volume of new work is started. This, in turn, will minimize the "hole" in the workflow and increase the volume through the shop.

Measure and Monitor Trends

Figure 9-1 shows a graph from a weekly management report that illustrates a gradually improving situation. Shipments during the first three weeks of each month are increasing while shipments during the fourth week (the spike) are declining.

Key Points

The term hockey stick refers to a typical pattern in job shops where a great effort is expended during the last week of the month to ship as much as possible to allow a company to make its numbers. Once established, the pattern is difficult to break, and causes additional production costs that are hidden and difficult to spot. It results from a combination of factors not a simple root cause.

The hockey stick is a dynamic organizational problem

Figure 9-1. A gradually improving hockey stick condition.

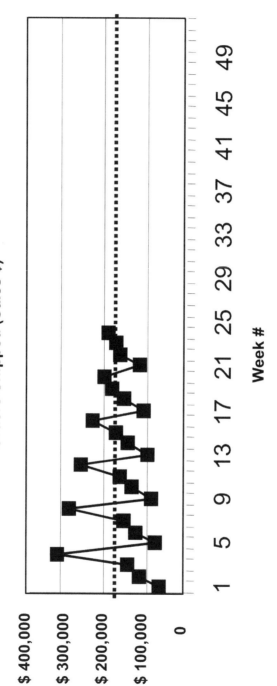
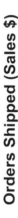

that cannot be solved by using a bold stroke. Therefore, it is necessary to:

◆ Understand the underlying dynamics.
◆ Change the company's perspective from monthly to weekly.
◆ Implement a weekly management report to track shipments and input volumes.
◆ Manage the entire business process.
◆ Adopt an incremental approach that yields a little progress at a time.

N O T E S

CHAPTER TEN

THE THORNY ISSUE OF JOB SHOP OVERHEAD

The question of how to allocate overhead is a thorny issue for many job shops. It is important because overhead is a significant portion of the cost structure, and consequently the price quoted to a customer. Using labor or machine hours as a basis for allocation is not always appropriate or accurate due to their variability.

The approach described in this chapter is to recognize overhead as a type of usage tax customers pay over and above the cost of direct labor and materials. The critical question is how to ensure each customer pays his or her fair share. The limitations of traditional allocation bases—

labor and machine hours primarily—are discussed, and an approach based on sales revenues is presented. The intent is *not* to propose a single correct way or a standard method for allocating overhead since each shop is different, and there is likely no single best method that fits every company. Rather, the aim is to offer a useful perspective and approach for this common job shop problem.

Labor Hours

Using labor hours as a basis for allocating overhead has its origin in mass-production volume manufacturing where work-to-time standards are well-established, the amount of labor per unit of output is nearly constant, and volume is relatively stable. This is not how a job shop works. There are setups and changeovers that cause lost time. Short runs have a learning curve so an operator probably never gets to maximum speed, or the so-called standard. Production workers are reassigned to different orders depending upon changing priorities, which causes more lost time. Jobs are moved in the queue to accommodate good customers, and the floor is generally dynamic—or even chaotic—compared to a station-fill, volume-manufacturing operation.

Machine Hours

The problem with machine or work-center hours is similar. They change depending upon the order backlog and flow of work through the shop. When you have a lot of work and high machine utilization, for example, the dollar amount of overhead carried per machine hour would be less because more machine hours are being used.

When orders are down, the opposite occurs. Does this mean that you lower your price when you have a surplus of work in the shop because the amount of overhead per machine hour is less? Or that you increase your price when volume is down? I don't think so.

Materials

Although materials are rarely considered as a basis for allocation, it would seem appropriate in some cases given that converting raw materials is the core process of manufacturing businesses and how value is created. The problem with this approach is that it depends on the type of production. One shop may be making a large number of small parts with high machine time, low materials usage, and moderate labor hours (for example, using operators as machine tenders), while another shop may have high materials costs (industrial pressure vessels, for example, which are huge and use thick steel) with low machine time, and a great amount of labor hours for planners, fitters, welders, grinders, assemblers, inspectors, and shippers. These situations are not comparable, which casts doubt on using materials as a *universal* basis for allocating overhead. However, it may be sufficient for determining facilities usage in certain shops, and certainly should be considered.

The Market Doesn't Care

It is important to recognize that the market ultimately determines the price. Customers compare your quote to a competitors' on the basis of price, lead time, quality, and reliability. They really don't care how you apportion the components of that price, such as labor, materials, overhead, and margin. You may feel comfortable using some type of job-costing method to substantiate a price, but from the market's point of view, this is non-value-adding activity.

Also, pricing is not an exact science. It is not a matter of merely adding up the direct costs of labor and materials, allocating an amount for overhead, and adding a margin. Your quote also depends on subjective factors: what you think the market will bear; your order backlog, because a shop will sometimes take low or no margin work to cover ongoing overhead expenses when business is down; the customer, since good customers may get preferential pricing; and other considerations.

Defining Overhead

Some companies go through a complicated accounting exercise to determine the breakdown of overhead between the shop and the rest of the business, or between fixed and semivariable costs. This probably isn't necessary for pricing because the customer ultimately foots the entire bill. *Overhead* is defined for our purposes here as "all the costs of the business with the exception of direct labor and materials used for a particular customer's order." The customer is expected to pay for the labor and materials for his order of course, plus his fair share of the overhead.

Fair-Share Concept

It is important to recognize that overhead is the cost of sustaining the organization so that it is available when the customer needs service. The allocation of any customer's fair share of the overhead should be based on use of the facility. Overhead is similar to a usage tax. The more a customer uses a *facility*, the more he or she should pay toward its overhead costs. The word facility is used here to refer to the entire organization and its costs, not only factory overhead. The underlying question is how to define *usage* of the facility before determining a customer's fair share.

This highlights the problem of using labor or machine hours or materials since these may or may not be representative of usage. Some orders take more labor than others, but why should a customer pay more for facilities usage, or in other words, pay a higher overhead rate? Some orders require more highly skilled people. Does this represent a greater use of the facility, and should the customer be expected to pay more? Not only does this appear to be an administrative nightmare, but labor, machine hours, and materials are not necessarily representative of facility usage. Before you know it, you're in a quagmire of numbers and have lost sight of the basic idea, which is to charge customers their fair share of the costs of the facility based on their usage of it. This is the primary objective of my overhead allocation method.

Allocating Usage

A fair way to allocate usage would be on the basis of sales dollars, which is an objective measure, not an estimate. The more dollars shipped to a customer, the higher the usage and the more overhead that customers should pay. Although this is an objective measure of usage, the problem is the catch-22 of needing the overhead allocation to add to the materials, labor, and margin to determine the quote price.

However, using sales dollars as a measure of usage provides a good rule of thumb, as well as a means for testing the accuracy of other allocation methods. The procedure is straightforward:

◆ Take your actual sales revenue for the previous twelve months and divide this by the number of orders shipped during this period. This will give you an average order size in sales dollars. For example, if you had $5 million in sales and shipped 2,250 orders (or 45 per week), the average order size would be $2,200.

◆ Next, take your total overhead expenses for the year and divide this by the number of orders to get the amount of overhead that must be carried by an average order. Remember, this is the total of all costs plus profits excluding direct materials and direct labor. For example, if materials and labor represent 35 percent of the cost, the balance of 65 percent ($3,250,000) would represent total overhead, which includes profit earned. Thus, the average overhead per order would be $1,400.

Table 10-1 summarizes these calculations.

Table 10-1. Calculations for an average order's overhead.

Sales Revenue	Orders Shipped	Average Order Size	Direct Labor & Materials	Total Overhead	Average Order's Overhead
$5,000,000	2,250	$2,200	$1,750,000	$3,250,000	$1,400

Calculating Overhead for an Average Order

Once you run through these simple calculations, you have the amount of overhead an average order needs to carry. This exercise can be clarifying, and you can use this number in several ways. For example, it functions as a rule of thumb that you can use to adjust overhead depending upon the size of the order. Larger orders obviously must carry more overhead. You can approximate overhead charges based on how a particular order or RFQ compares to the average.

Another option is to add estimated direct labor and materials costs, and then add an overhead amount based on the cost of maintaining the facility. For example, suppose that direct labor and materials amount to 35 percent of your sales, so the remaining 65 percent would include all other costs of doing business plus your profit margin. An average order of $2,200 would require $770 for materials and labor plus $1,430 for overhead costs and profit. This can be calculated as follows: $770/0.35 = $2,200.

You can also use it as a sanity check to test other allocation methods you may develop for your shop. You can experiment with a mix of labor hours, machine hours, and/or materials usage to construct an index that is representative of facilities usage. If this method tracks to the average derived from these calculations, you can be reasonably certain that you have a fair method for determining facilities usage and charging customers their fair share of overhead.

Monitoring Performance

Odd as it may seem, if you win too high a percentage of bids, this may be a problem because it could be an indication that your prices are too low. Monitoring the dollars won and comparing them to bids won will give you an indication of how well you are faring in the market-place. For example, one company found they were winning about 40 percent of the RFQs quoted, but only 20 percent of the dollars. They concluded they were winning all the "junk" that nobody else wanted. This conclusion led them to rethinking their strategy and approach to their market.

In sum, allocating overhead in a job shop environment is a thorny issue for many companies. Using labor or machine hours or materials as a basis may not be an appropriate or accurate representation of facilities usage. An alternative approach is to use sales dollars as a measure of usage, determine the amount of overhead associated with an average order, and then construct an index that tracks to this average.

The temptation is to assume there is one best way for calculating and allocating overhead costs that applies universally to all shops. An alternative is to find the best way to define and measure usage for your shop, which is based on the specifics of production and industry practices. There may not be an ideal way to determine overhead allocation, but there may be a way that will work adequately for you.

Key Points

◆ Seeing overhead as a usage tax that is charged to the customer puts the concept in a different perspective.

◆ It is important to recognize the difference between trying to find a way to define and measure facilities usage versus trying to find a way to allocate overhead. Usage is a concept, while allocating overhead is a method. The concept should come first.

◆ When you can define and quantify usage of a facility, calculating the amount a customer uses and his or her fair share of the overhead cost should be straightforward.

◆ Calculating an average order's overhead charge can be used to assess the suitability and accuracy of other methods.

◆ There may not be a single best way for determining facilities usage and allocation of overhead that is applicable to all shops. However, there may be a method that is adequate based on the specifics of your business.

NOTES

CHAPTER ELEVEN

THE BIG PICTURE PERSPECTIVE

Everyone knows that sales and profits are the funda-mental measures of business performance, and a seri-ous concern of business owners and chief executives. What is not so clear, however, is how changes in the *relationship* between these key indices are monitored and interpreted. The matrix in Figure 11-1 provides a convenient way to broadly assess and interpret the performance of a business by contrasting changes in sales revenues and profits over time.

Four basic scenarios are described. Each has significant implications for business strategy and performance-improvement programming. When built into the man-agement report and tracked consistently, the matrix provides a reliable method for assessing the vitality of your business and for quickly alerting you to danger signs before a situation reaches the crisis stage. It is important to recognize that all scenarios are short-term and transitional. There is no "steady state" in a business.

Scenario 1

Both sales and profits are growing. This scenario suggests a basically healthy organization that has the ability to serve more demand with no increase in total costs.

A variation on this theme would be profits growing at a greater rate than sales, which suggests that the organization has the capacity to serve increased demand with greater efficiently. When overhead or fixed costs are spread out or absorbed by greater volume with no increase in unit costs, profit will grow at a faster rate than sales.

Warning Sign

Conversely, if profit is increasing, but at a lesser rate than sales, this suggests some organizational limits are being pushed and inefficiencies are being encountered. Alternatively, it could mean the company has invested in additional infrastructure to support anticipated growth in demand, but this additional sales demand has not yet fully materialized.

Scenario 2

In this case, revenues are falling and profits are rising. This scenario suggests serious cost cutting may be underway, likely through downsizing or by cutting fixed costs and overhead. It could also mean products have been

Figure 11-1. Quad Matrix

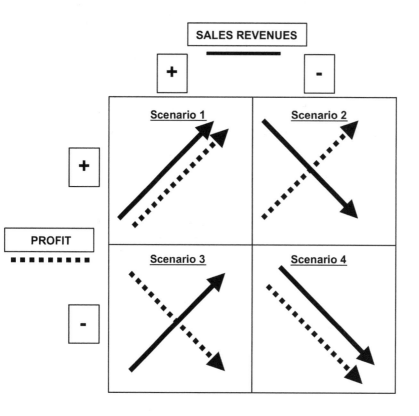

redesigned, or more efficient production processes have been put in place. This scenario could also result from selling off unprofitable businesses or pruning unprofitable customers.

This is only a short-term strategy, however. Cost cutting can buy the business some time to work on increasing sales, or if this is not feasible, to resize the organization so that costs are in line with sales, making the business profitable at a lower volume level. In most cases, it is very difficult for management to cut costs faster than revenues are declining.

Scenario 3

In this scenario, revenues are increasing and profits are decreasing. The organization is not able to process additional demand profitably, which suggests a lack of adequate infrastructure and related organizational problems. Chaos and confusion can result when an organization is under pressure to meet increasing demand that it cannot handle, resulting in waste and higher costs. This scenario may indicate that pricing is too low or the company is buying market share. This may be a legitimate business strategy, but it needs to be investigated.

Scenario 4

This is obviously the worst-case scenario because both revenues and profits are declining. Major work is required to address sales and profit deterioration. The organization may choose to transition to Scenario 2 with a cost-cutting strategy and program, thereby buying some time to address sales issues that require more time to see results, since cost cutting can usually be accomplished more quickly than building sales.

This revenue-profit matrix provides a useful framework for understanding an organizational situation quickly. Locating your business in one of the quadrants provides a "quick and dirty" method for gaining a basic understanding of your situation so that you can formulate new strategies and focus on improvement programming. All business states are transitional, so continually monitoring the revenue-profit relationship will alert you to changes sooner. As a result, you can take appropriate actions before a situation deteriorates further.

N O T E S

CHAPTER TWELVE

WHAT BUSINESS ARE YOU REALLY IN?

If buggy whip manufacturers had seen themselves in the "motivation business," would they have been able to adapt and survive in the automobile age? We've all heard that if the railroads had seen themselves in the transportation business, they would have been able to recognize and exploit opportunities in air travel and trucking instead of being clobbered by these new industries. A similar case could be made for mainframe computer makers when the PC came on the scene.

It's essential for any company to have a clear understanding of the question, "What business are we really in?" In fact, answering this deceptively simple question may be one of the *most* important things you can do to ensure that your company is positioned to grow and prosper.

The Need for Conceptual Space

A well-conceived, clearly stated definition provides the conceptual space and strategic insight necessary to guide a company's future direction. This is especially important in today's turbulent business environment where whole industries seem to appear and disappear virtually overnight. The ability to adapt to change and the impact of new technologies is an absolute business requirement for every company.

However, answering this question in a way that will provide strategic insight and direction is not easy. Many companies, perhaps even a large majority, either ignore the question entirely, or have an answer that misses the mark as the following story illustrates.

Case Example

It seems that a well-known management consultant was asked to assist a declining manufacturer of glass bottles. After taking a look around the plant, the consultant asks the President, "What business are you in?"

"We're in the bottle-making business, of course."

"No, you're not! You're in the packaging business!"

And with this one stroke of insight, the consultant opened up new possibilities and growth opportunities for this failing company. With management's thinking no longer limited by glass bottles, they could expand into the broader world of packaging, use other materials in addition to glass, seek new customers, and focus on new markets. In fact, recognizing that a primary function of packaging is to sell products, they might even consider adding a design service to assist customers in developing more powerful packaging.

Guidelines

Any company that chooses to address this basic business question can benefit from these guidelines:

◆ Look at your company from the outside in—from the point of view of customers, potential customers, and markets to serve. Ask: "What are they really buying from us and why?" Don't overlook the fact that a job shop is a service business.

◆ Look at your company from a *functional perspective* as opposed to the physical—packaging as opposed to bottle-making, motivation as opposed to buggy-whips, transportation as opposed to trains, information management as opposed to computers, fasteners as opposed to nuts and bolts, power transmission as opposed to gear-making, metal enclosures as opposed to fuse boxes or file cabinets, fluid power transmission as opposed to hydraulic valves and couplings.

◆ Understanding the difference between physical products and functional utility. This is essential. According to value engineering guru Richard Park, a functional definition should be simple, short (two or three words), and open up creative opportunities for the company (for example, "We're in the packaging business.")

◆ Be careful not to make your functional definition too broad, as this will cause you to lose focus. For example, if the bottle-making company defined itself as being in the *container business*, this would have opened up too many impractical possibilities beyond their capabilities (for example, overseas shipping containers).

◆ Don't be afraid to think in larger, more abstract terms—in outlines instead of overwhelming, mind-numbing detail. A major predicament any company can encounter here is the old problem of not being able to see the forest for the trees. *It is possible to have too much information!*

Organic Organizational Model

Odd as this may seem, redefining your company's conceptual space is a bit like repotting a plant. If you pick the next larger-size pot, the plant will grow and flourish. But if the pot is too large, the plant will not respond in the same vigorous manner. In this case, packaging is the right size pot; containers are too large.

Product-Service Packages

It can be helpful to think in terms of product-service packages when you are considering the value your company offers to customers. For example, customers may actually be buying problem solutions (i.e., your company's creativity, engineering talent, years of experience), additional production capacity (without having to invest in capital expansion), quick response time (vs. poor service from internal production), cost avoidance or savings, cash flow relief (for example, your credit policy), or your company's on-time delivery reliability.

Rethinking a company's business concept is an important new area in the management of organizations since the methodology and tools required to bring about this type of conceptual redefinition are now available. Pioneering research shows how new paradigms supplant obsolete thinking in organizations, and systems dynamics yields rich new perspectives. These advances enable a systematic approach to the work of conceptual redefinition as a real possibility. A qualified outsider can be most helpful here because this work requires a different perspective and set of skills compared to those needed for the day-to-day management of an organization or company.

A Caveat

Redefining a company's business along new lines is a creative process that does not lend itself completely to a "facts and rules" approach. Sometimes it takes a period of time, thought, and struggle to wrest a new perspective and interpretation from a situation. But when you hit the right construct, the results can be outstanding in terms of the creativity and energy released within an organization. The resulting growth is certainly well worth the effort.

Just how valuable is the ability to reconceptualize a faltering business to give it a new lease on life? One can only wonder what might have happened if buggy-whip makers saw gasoline as the "motivation" for a car.

NOTES

PART III

APPENDIXES: TOOLS OF THE TRADE

IS THIS YOUR SHOP?

Fill out this questionnaire and see how *Speed to Market* can have a positive impact on your business. Check *Yes* or *No* in the box located on the right side of each statement. Refer to the item analysis that follows to see how reducing lead time can help correct the problem areas you have indicated.

Is This Your Shop?	Y	N
1. Our customers want it all: price, quality, and fast delivery.		
2. Customers constantly change priorities, causing confusion and adding cost.		
3. We are continually rescheduling orders in production.		
4. We need to increase sales—competition is fierce.		
5. We're uncertain about the accuracy of our estimates.		
6. Our lead times are too long.		
7. WIP is too high and there are too many orders on the floor at one time.		
8. Rework is killing us.		
9. A psychological wall exists between the office and shop.		
10. We seem to have the same problems over and over.		
11. Setups and changeovers take too long.		
12. We don't know whether we make or lose money on orders.		
13. We continually ship late.		
14. Getting accurate information for analysis and decision making is a nightmare.		
15. Cash flow is a constant problem.		

Item Analysis

1. *Our customers want it all: price, quality, and fast delivery.* Par for the course. Typical demands being placed on suppliers in a just-in-time manufacturing world.

2. *Customers constantly change priorities, causing confusion and adding costs.* It is a given that customers will always want orders more quickly and will change delivery dates. Responding to these requests means that you must reschedule and juggle orders already in production, which creates confusion and adds costs. However, reducing lead time can satisfy customers' expectations of what is reasonable, for example, a three-week lead time may be reasonable whereas three months is excessive. It also reduces the window of opportunity for changes. For example, a shop that can deliver in three weeks instead of an industry standard of twelve will have effectively eliminated 75 percent of the time during which a customer may request a schedule change.

3. *We are continually rescheduling orders in production.* Insofar as rescheduling results from customers' requesting new delivery dates, this problem will be dramatically reduced by having shorter lead times for the reasons mentioned above. However, there may be other causes for constant rescheduling, such as late component deliveries from your suppliers or overscheduling the plant. These must be investigated and corrected as part of any lead-time reduction program.

4. *We need to increase sales—competition is fierce.* There is no question that speed is a competitive advantage when it comes to winning bids. This is especially true when little difference exists among

competitors' prices and quality. Custom manufacturing is essentially a service business. When you reduce the amount of time customers must wait to have their needs met, you can expect more sales. If increasing sales is one of your company's objectives, faster deliver is the key, not cutting prices.

5. *We're unsure about the accuracy of our estimates.* Without accurate estimating, pricing is mere guesswork. If your pricing is too low, you'll leave money on the table and erode profits; if your pricing is too high, you'll lose sales. In either case, your business will suffer. The need to close the loop is discussed in Chapters 6 and 7. Streamlining and rationalizing the overall business process includes the ability to compare estimates to actual production costs. This provides the foundation for continuous improvement, as well as upgrading essential information used in estimating.

6. *Our lead times are too long.* Even if your lead times are not overly long, you should be actively working to serve your customers more quickly by relentlessly focusing on cutting lead time.

7. *WIP is too high and there are too many orders on the floor at one time.* This can be a symptom of many factors: the shop is being overscheduled; excessive rework is eating up otherwise productive capacity; constantly rescheduling and reprioritizing orders causes confusion; delays from external parts or subassembly vendors prevents orders from being completed; and more. These are the kinds of problems that a lead-time reduction program will enable your people to identify and correct.

8. *Rework is killing us.* Excessive rework is one of the most expensive forms of waste in any manufacturing operation, and many reasons cause it. The lead-time reduction program described in this book incorporates a continuous improvement cycle that will enable you to pinpoint problems and develop effective solutions.

9. *A psychological wall or barrier exists between the office and the shop.* This is a common complaint in many organizations and a chief cause of problems and poor performance. Business literacy, or a shared understanding of how your business actually works, combined with a unifying focus on the goal of reducing lead time will lower barriers, improve communications, and promote teamwork. This is one reason why it is essential to encompass the total business process and include everyone who has a key role to play in making this process work more effectively.

10. *We seem to be dealing with the same problems over and over.* See comments on rework, continuous improvement, organization communications, and other related items.

11. *Set-ups and changeovers take too long.* A technique for reducing changeover time is described in Chapter 5.

12. *We don't know if we make or lose money on orders.* This requires the ability to compare estimated to actual costs on an order-by-order basis. See previous comments related to the accuracy of estimates in Chapter 6.

13. *We continually ship late.* There are a variety of dynamics involved. See previous items.

14. *Getting accurate information for analysis and decision making is a nightmare.* This scenario indicates fragmented systems, failure to close the loop, the shop floor's data-collection problems, and lack of continuous improvement methods. This problem can also be attacked directly as described in Chapter 6.
15. *Cash flow is a constant problem.* This is typical, especially in small shops. Cash flow will be greatly improved when lead times are reduced.

N O T E S

N O T E S

DETAILED VIEW OF A JOB SHOP BUSINESS PROCESS

Figure B-1 shows the flow of a typical job shop business process.

Explanatory Notes

1. Although job shops work on an order-by-order basis, it is important to have a company vision, business strategy, and plan for focusing activities and setting goals for the future.

2. The sales and marketing departments are focused on current and potential customers. Their mission is to promote awareness of a shop and its

Figure B-1. Flow of a typical job shop process.

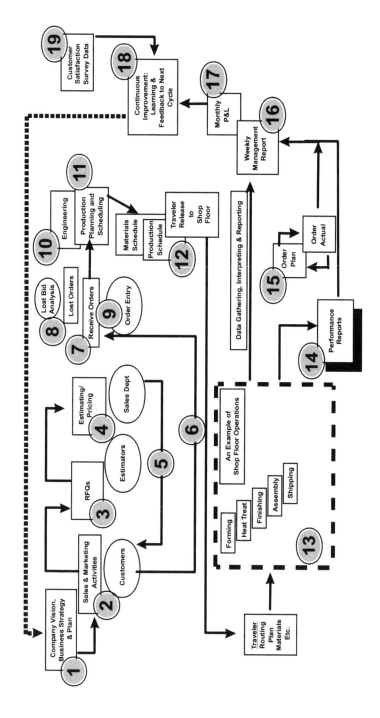

capabilities. Effectiveness can be measured in terms of RFQs generated, new customers secured, and growth.

3. RFQs result from sales and marketing activities and from repeat business.

4. Estimates and quotations are prepared in response to RFQs.

5. The sales force communicates quotes to customers.

6. Customers communicate acceptance or award to another vendor; follow-up is often required.

7. Shop receives results of bid; either gets order or not.

8. Losing bids are analyzed individually and collectively.

9. Orders are entered into shop's production process.

10. Engineering can be extensive or limited to shop drawing and specifications. Use a project scheduling system to ensure timely completion of engineering work in the overall process.

11. Production planning and scheduling includes a shop-floor router "package," materials acquisition, scheduling, and capacity planning. (Router preparation is the responsibility of engineering in some shops.)

12. Router provides product specifications and production information to shop floor.

13. Typical metal-working shop manufacturing process.

14. Various shop-floor performance reports, such as productivity, quality, scrap, rework, and on-time completion.

15. Closing the loop—comparing estimates to actual production costs and margin attainment.

16. Weekly management report captures and summarizes key operational and financial data; if these are acceptable, profit and loss (P&L) will be favorable, thus enabling management to see and respond to problems quickly.

17. Monthly profit-and-loss statement.

18. Continuous improvement facilitates learning, which improves performance on future orders.

19. Customer satisfaction survey data is used as an additional source of input into the continuous improvement loop.

NOTES

NOTES

NOTES

N O T E S

HOW TO CONDUCT A BUSINESS SYSTEMS REVIEW

An enterprisewide process in a custom manufacturing environment starts with methods used by sales and marketing for generating opportunities to bid, all the way through the steps required to convert an RFQ into an order, an order into a shipment, and the resulting account receivable into cash and profits. It also includes the management tools necessary for running the business, such as planning documents and reports.

To conduct a system or process review, you must first make the process explicit before you can critique and improve it. The problem is that these routines are hidden in your business, having become part of the woodwork so to speak. For example, every department either generates new forms—that is, creates a router prior to an order being released to the shop or creates an invoice—or modifies paperwork or digital information—such as relieving raw materials inventory or changing an accounts-receivable balance. They also keep some form of records and accounts for their own purposes, which can be a vast hidden bureaucracy that serves its own needs as opposed to serving the needs of the business. The solution is to make it explicit and visual so that it can be reviewed in total.

Note: An enterprisewide business systems review differs in some respects from the process-step value analysis. For example, the process-step value analysis focuses on the physical production of the product on the floor or the accomplishment of work in general, whereas the business systems review focuses on the management system and paperwork. However, the same value-adding perspective and questions are applicable to both.

Step 1

These system flows can be quite large and the best way that I have seen to make them explicit is through what has been termed "the brown paper." This procedure involves fastening a roll of brown wrapping paper on a long wall and then taping to it all the forms you use in running your business. These forms should be logically arranged to correspond with the overall business process.

These process flows can reach thirty feet or more in length, three- to six-feet high, depending upon complexity. Everyone participates because everyone plays some part in the system. Hanging the brown paper on a long wall in public view attracts attention and interest. This is a great way to gain employee input and involvement. Encourage people to question the way things are done and to make recommendations. This involvement will be helpful later when everyone needs to play an active role in actually implementing changes and improvements.

Step 2

Once the business system is clearly illustrated, the next step is to review each step to identify opportunities for improvement. Assemble everyone in the organization who plays a key role in the process, including managers and supervisors. Walk through the process flow step by step. Ask each person to explain his or her function and activities: where their work comes from, what they do with it, where do they send it when it's finished, what problems are they experiencing, what would make it easier, faster, and so forth. Note problems and opportunities for improvement by writing them on the paper or on Post-it® notes, which can be attached to the paper.

Make certain that each step serves the next downstream operation as effectively and efficiently as possible. For example, where the office is responsible for preparing a shop-floor information package, is it clear, complete, readable, accurate, and timely? If not, problems, delays, and added costs can occur during production. Each step in the process must be reviewed and downstream operations must state their requirements as "internal customers."

Step 3

Define the performance expectations for each step in the process, which can be both qualitative and quantitative. For example, you may find that it takes too much time to prepare estimates and communicate bids to customers. You can set a performance expectation for this activity— for example, all RFQs must be turned around in twenty-four hours—and then focus on achieving this goal consistently. Later you can establish acceptable costs per unit of output. Brainstorm ways to reduce the time required for each step. Pay particular attention to unnecessary delays within and between process steps. Reducing process-step time is the key to reducing overall company lead time. Remember the two types of time: process time and task time.

Step 4

Once this systems review is complete, you will have accomplished several objectives:

◆ You now have a new perspective and a great deal of information about how your business actually works on a day-to-day basis. This can be a real eye-opener for management.

◆ Key people in your organization are now much more knowledgeable about the business and their function within it. As a result, they can work together more effectively and do their jobs with greater understanding and skill.

◆ You have a list of problems, opportunities for improvement, and some innovative ideas in hand.

◆ You will have a good sense of priorities—what to tackle first, second, and so on. Keep in mind, though, that it is often better to solve less difficult problems first, even though the impact may be modest, as opposed to plunging into a high-return issue that will be very difficult or costly to implement.

◆ You have generated energy and enthusiasm for change that now must be channeled into action and results.

Step 5

Implement changes and improvements. The outcome of any review must be acted upon and change implemented before any measurable results will be attained.

Note: Some people think computer process–mapping programs are better than the hands-on brown paper technique described previously, but I don't find this to be the case. Computer process–mapping software can show you the steps and substeps in the process, but it is an abstraction of the process and, therefore, misses the substance of the real thing. The brown paper lets you see the actual form filled out. The computer will only tell you that a form is filled out at that point. Also, the information used to create the computer map is provided by people in the organization who think they know what happens at each step—what they think may or may not be the case. The other disadvantage of computer process–mapping is that it doesn't involve your people or build upon their skills. The brown paper, on the other hand, is an *event* in which many people participate in and contribute to in a meaningful way.

N O T E S

N O T E S

N O T E S

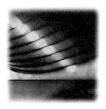

HOW TO CONDUCT A PROCESS-STEP VALUE ANALYSIS

A process-step value analysis is a technique for looking at work processes and finding ways to improve them. This tool can be applied to sales, estimating, clerical work, or any process within an organization. It is described here in terms of its application to the shop floor.

The basic idea is to look at everything that happens to an order as it actually progresses through the shop. There are several objectives:

◆ To identify those activities that add value and those that do not. *Value adding* can be defined as anything that changes the physical form or appearance of the product

◆ To eliminate non-value-adding activities

◆ To reduce the time required to perform value-adding activities

◆ To reduce the delay time between activities

◆ To increase business literacy, that is, to educate organization members in how the business actually works

The technique itself is straightforward. A group of people representing various functions and departments is assembled. They follow the progress of an order through the sequence of operations on the floor. One member of the team writes every activity performed on a task/activity analysis worksheet, and another person counts the walking steps from one operation to another to determine travel distances.

The group as a whole makes collective decisions as to whether or not a particular task or activity adds value from the customer's point of view, which usually can be easily determined. No changes or decisions are made at this time because it is only a fact-finding process at this stage.

Once the walk-through has been completed, the group analyzes every step using the process critique guide. Group members look for opportunities to eliminate tasks, combine them with other operations or tasks, change methods or tools, reduce distances traveled, or enhance skills via training. Once these decisions have been made, the next step is to implement these recommendations on the floor. This is where many programs falter because management is often reluctant to make significant changes. However, dramatic opportunities for improvement often require drastic measures such as moving machines out of their previous life-long locations into another area that better suits the process flow, rather than grouping all similar machines together. Once employees see these kinds of changes happening, they know management is serious about improvement.

The following four tools are necessary for performing this analysis:

1. Task/activity data collection procedure
2. Task/activity data collection worksheet
3. Process critique guide
4. Results summary

Task/Activity Data Collection Procedure
Purpose

The purpose of the task/activity data collection procedure is to provide an organized method for documenting and describing the steps in a work process.

Procedure

Assemble a cross-functional team and follow the progress of an order through the shop. One person documents each task or activity on this form. Another person counts the walking steps from one task or activity to the next (one step = approximately 2.5 feet).

Make an initial determination on this walk-through whether a task or activity adds value or not. *Value adding* is defined as anything that changes the physical form or

appearance of the product. The examples in Table D-1
include:

Cutting	Counting
Heat Treat	Recounting
Grinding	Moving
Drilling	Storing
Boring	Removing from Storage
Honing	Stacking
Polishing	Unstacking
Packing	Inspecting
Shipping	Scheduling

Table D-1. Examples of value-adding and non–value-adding activities.

Value-Adding	Non–Value-Adding
Cutting	Counting
Heat Treat	Recounting
Grinding	Moving
Drilling	Storing
Boring	Removing from Storage
Honing	Stacking
Polishing	Unstacking
Packing	Inspecting
Shipping	Scheduling

Engage the operators and employees in the process. Don't be afraid to ask why a particular activity is performed, or why it is performed in a certain way. It is important for team members to be purposefully ignorant of shop-floor operations so that everyone feels comfortable asking questions. In fact, it can be useful to include a team member or two who is totally unfamiliar with manufacturing processes to ask the so-called dumb questions.

Recognize that there are two types of time—task time and process or throughput time—and that time can be measured in minutes, hours, days, or weeks. For example, it may only take a few minutes to perform a particular task, but it may take days before the order moves from one operation to the next. Time estimates are based on reasonable expectancies, not precise calculations. In other words, don't go out on the floor with a stopwatch.

After you have completed gathering data and the worksheet (see next page) is complete, the group meets to analyze, discuss, and decide on which actions to take (see the "Process Critique Guide" section of this appendix).

Task/Activity Data Collection Worksheet

Task/Activity Description	Add Value?	Time	Steps
Totals			

Process Critique Guide

Purpose

The purpose of the process critique guide is to provide team members with a ready reference for the types of questions to ask when analyzing process steps. The overall objective is to eliminate unnecessary time consumption within and between tasks or activities.

Questions to Ask

- Can the task or activity be eliminated completely?
- Can improvement be realized by changing the physical location of the task?
- Can improvement be realized by changing the sequence of the task in the overall manufacturing process?
- Can improvement be realized by upgrading the skills of the operator or changing the person performing the task or activity?
- What is the purpose of this step?
- Where are we doing it here?
- When do we do it?
- Who does it?
- Are there other people doing the same thing?
- Can it be outsourced more efficiently?
- Could we do it at another time?
- Can someone else do it?
- Can it be combined?
- Is there some other way to do it?

Evaluation

Evaluate each improvement alternative in terms of volume, quality, task time savings, process or throughput time compression, and cost savings. The revised work process should yield the greatest volume of work, at an acceptable quality level, in the least amount of time. The details of this critique are recorded on the results summary (see next page).

Note: Recognize that no measurable savings will be realized without implementing the team's recommendations.

Results Summary

Task/Activity	Action to Be Taken	Estimated Savings	
		Time	Steps
Current Totals from Task/ Activity Data Collection Worksheet			
New Totals after Critique			
Savings/Improvement			

N O T E S

NOTES

NOTES

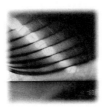

DYNAMIC PROBLEM SOLVING

M any organizational problems do not yield to linear, cause–effect analyses because they involve a number of elements that are interconnected in a larger system. It is critical to understand how these dynamics work before you try to solve a problem. Most often, a resolution requires multiple solution strategies, not a single change.

Dynamic problem solving involves identifying the elements in the larger problem system and mapping their interactive relationships. The technique is straightforward:

- ◆ Cover a wall with white wrapping paper or use a white board.
- ◆ Convene a group of people who have a stake in

solving the problem and the organizational clout to implement a solution.

◆ Appoint a facilitator to keep the group on track.

◆ Map the problem dynamics using colored markers to illustrate elements and their interactive influences.

◆ Determine how the dynamics in the system can be altered.

◆ Decide what needs to be done.

◆ Implement the necessary actions.

Case Example

When dynamic problem solving was used to address a chronic turnover problem in a factory, it revealed complex dynamics that are illustrated in the map in Figure E-1. This map enabled management to view the entire situation at one time and to gain perspective on the broader, long-term implications of this problem for the business. It enabled them to see turnover as a business problem that resulted in profit erosion and long-term business deterioration, as opposed to being a personnel problem.

Solution strategies included:

◆ Eliminating the piecework system

◆ Bringing wages in line with prevailing rates in the area

◆ Reducing the probationary time period—new employees get raises sooner

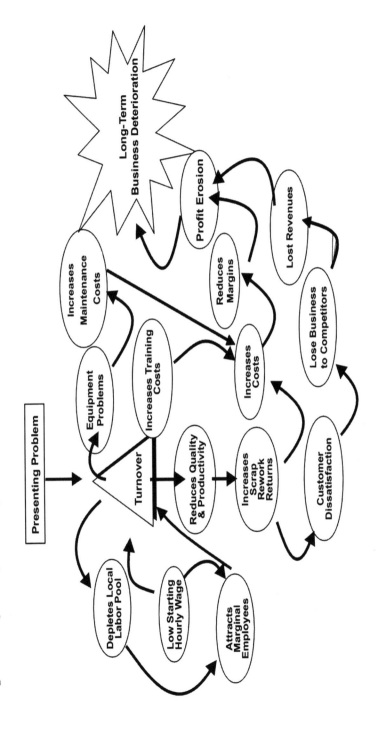

Figure E-1. Dynamics of a turnover problem.

◆ Implementing a shopwide productivity bonus program
◆ Creating a more formal training program
  combined with a buddy system

N O T E S

N O T E S

DRAWING THE NEW ORGANIZATION LINES: INFORMATION TECHNOLOGY AS THE NEW ORGANIZATION STRUCTURE

The new organization lines being drawn today are not the lines and boxes of traditional organization charts. Rather they are the information flows, databases, and communications linkages required to support mission critical and other related organization processes. As process and value-adding thinking become more widespread in organizations, information technology (IT) will play a more central role in organization design. When it is well designed and effectively implemented, information technology offers tremendous potential for improving any organization's competitiveness, as well as providing a solid foundation for future growth and profitability.

Information Technology Is the New Organization Structure

Organization processes are dynamic, broad in scope, and operate continuously in real time. They cross individual functions, often extending into the organizations of both customers and suppliers. This tendency makes organizational processes difficult to manage by using traditional methods. A process-oriented organization is not managed in the same manner as a pyramid hierarchy. This is one reason why there is a need for seamless and self-organizing processes. Information technology, not the organization chart, provides the structure for process integration, alignment, and self-regulation.

The Benefits of IT Are Not Being Realized

However, the effective use of information technology requires more than merely knowing the technical capabilities of IT systems and being able to hook them together. Research conducted at the Massachusetts

Institute of Technology and reported by Robert Benjamin and Eliot Levinson in the *Sloan Management Review*[1] supports this conclusion:

> *The benefits of IT are not being realized because investment is heavily biased towards technology and not towards managing changes in process and organization structure and culture. Elsewhere they state: As most managers realize, new technology is not enough to increase productivity. Organizational and process changes must also be made. Managers must know how to integrate the technology, business processes, and organization in order to achieve the goals they expect with the technology.*

Linking IT and Organization Design

Research and practical experience support the judgment that information technology alone is not sufficient for achieving maximum results. Information technology solutions must be designed in the context of a broader plan for improvement that is based on a thorough understanding of the business, competitive environment, organization, and future outlook. The design perspective proceeds from the broader value chain, or higher level system, in which every organization operates. Critical performance elements must be recognized and integrated into an overall plan for improvement. This will enable IT installations to be more productive and to have a greater impact on bottom-line business results.

What Is Organization Design?

Traditionally, *organization design* is defined as "organization structure." Historically, the emphasis has been on questions of centralization versus decentralization, or whether geography, products, functions, customers, market segments, or even time frames should be used to configure an enterprise. More recently, however, leading practitioners in the field recognize that an organization's structure is not a stand-alone design element. Structure cannot be separated from business strategy, management planning, mission-critical processes, information systems, culture, or people. An organization must be designed from "whole cloth," so to speak.

What Is Information Technology?

Information technology can be either broadly or narrowly defined. Definitions can range from automating a portion of a process to increase efficiency and reduce costs to the broader view of information technology as organization structure. There is probably no single definition of IT that would satisfy everyone. Regardless of how it may be defined, however, IT is a burgeoning technology that can have a tremendous impact on any company's performance, profitability, and future prosperity.

Structure Is Not a Stand Alone Design Element—And Neither Is IT

From an organization-design point of view, information technology must be considered in the context of an enterprisewide perspective. It is a critical element that must be integrated into an overall approach for building any company's competitiveness and profitability. Maximum results come when information technology is designed into the larger business and organizational context, rather than being superimposed upon it. In the right hands, the perspective, concepts, and methodology of organization design and information technology represent a powerful enterprisewide approach for improving an organization's performance and enhancing its future viability.

The Goals of Organization Design and IT Are Essentially the Same

A successful result is an enterprise that clearly understands its mission and strategic direction, is better positioned competitively in its environment now and for the future, adapts to change more easily, and operates more efficiently and effectively.

How to Integrate Organization Design and Information Technology

The integration of IT and organization design begins during the proposal stage of any prospective project. This is when the scope is defined and the preliminary project approach formulated. A proposal that proceeds from an organization-design framework is guaranteed to be stronger and more comprehensive—and likely more salable to management—than an IT proposal prepared without it.

In the *Harvard Business Review*, Peter Drucker laid out the following challenge:

> *Now we are entering a third period of change: the shift from the command-and-control organization, the organization of departments and divisions, to the information-based organization, the organization of knowledge specialists. We can perceive, though perhaps only dimly, what this organization will look like. We can identify some of its main characteristics and requirements. We can point to central problems of values, struc-*

ture, and behavior. But the job of actually building the information-based organization is still ahead of us—it is the managerial challenge of the future.[2]

The Bottom Line

Companies are better served when the benefits and positive impact of new information technology are maximized. Linking organization design and IT is an effective strategy for achieving this objective.

References

1. Robert I. Benjamin and Eliot Levinson, "A Framework for Managing IT-Enabled Change," *Sloan Management Review*, Summer 1993, pp. 23–33.
2. Peter F. Drucker, "The Coming of the New Organization," *Harvard Business Review*, January-February 1988, pp. 45–53.

N O T E S

N O T E S

INDEX

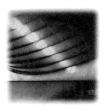

ABOUT THE
AUTHOR

Vincent Bozzone has generated millions of dollars in new revenues and earnings for companies as a result of his ability to conceive, plan, and implement solutions for a broad range of strategic and operating problems. He is the president of Delta Dynamics Incorporated, a firm he founded in 1991 to provide job shops and custom manufacturers with expertise and hands-on implementation support to improve performance and profitability in a lean manufacturing world. He has written many articles for professional journals and business publications, a chapter in the *Handbook of Organizational Consultation*, and two books on international business. He is an MBA graduate of Columbia University, the Past

President of the Association for the Management of Organization Design, and lives in Bloomfield Hills, Michigan. For more information, visit www.deltadynamicsinc.com.